PARDON
MY QUIRK

Anecdotes to make you
LAUGH, LEARN and **THINK**

Mo Barrett

Publishing Services provided by Paper Raven Books

Printed in the United States of America

First Printing, 2021

Hardback ISBN= 978-1-7354465-2-3
Paperback ISBN= 978-1-7354465-3-0

Praise for *Pardon My Quirk*

She stops time.

Psst…That's a compliment.

I'm standing in the back of the room at an event I am running.

I'm not sure who I like watching more—seeing her own the crowd like a magician dazzling her spectators or watching the audience watch her while truly hanging on every word, innuendo and metaphor.

I don't normally interrogate my attendees, yet I beeline over to her because I have to know…

"How long have you been a professional speaker?"

I've only spoken a few times.

"Theatre background?"

Unless you consider a 25-year Air Force career theatrical, um no.

"Extensive storytelling training?"

Except for listening to my dad's endless stories, also no.

Most people spend years and years and even more years to learn how to captivate an audience like you do.

Don't ever stop telling your stories.

Because when you tell them, time stands still for us.

—KYMBERLEE WEIL,
STORYTELLING AND SPEAKING STRATEGIST,
STORYTELLING SCHOOL

Mo, the monosyllabic-monikered author leverages laughter for levity and lighthearted lessons. As they say, hindsight is 20/20 and her anecdotes viewed through the lens of humor help any reader find the funny in everyday spectacles. But that's not all. She widens the aperture beyond the laugh, helping you learn from every interaction, giving you something to think about and prompting you to see the humor in your own life. No need to pardon her quirk, these anecdotes DO make you laugh, learn and think.

—ANDREW TARVIN,
FOUNDER AND CEO, HUMOR THAT WORKS

Barrett stunningly delivers on all her literary promises. Must read? BIG HUGE CHECK.

—RANDALL KENNETH JONES,
HOST, JONES.SHOW PODCAST

When I first met Mo Barrett a little over a year ago, I was impressed with her wit and intellect. You can't help but feel cheerful in her presence. She has a remarkable ability to extract wisdom from what most people see as just mundane everyday events. In her book *Pardon My Quirk*, she uses an easy storytelling style to share some of these gems with us. As a fellow U.S. Air Force officer, I could relate to many of the situations she shares in the book. I found myself nodding, smiling, and laughing through every page!

—General Ellen Pawlikowski,
U.S. Air Force, Retired

Pardon My Quirk is one of the funnest and most unexpected books of our time. Mo Barrett's unique storytelling and sharing of great life advice are uniquely shared in this wonderful compilation of short stories and lessons. Another great feature of this book is you can pick it up at any page and instantly be pulled into the story and lesson.

—Ken Sterling,
Executive Vice President, BigSpeak

Pardon My Quirk is the perfect collection of anecdotes from the life experiences of a truly unique person. Mo has put her own quirky twist on a modern version of *Aesop's Fables* meets *I Love Lucy*. Her self-deprecating humor is blended with heartfelt stories that make this book a fun read. With great leadership lessons throughout, Mo will get you to think about life from different perspectives while you quietly learn and laugh out loud.

—JIM VASELOPULOS,
CEO, RAFTI ADVISORS

Mo Barrett is one of a kind. I've been asking her to write this book for years. Well, she's finally done it and it's a doozy. *Pardon My Quirk* is filled with stories as only Mo can tell them. Funny and smart. I'm delighted by Mo's adventures and I'm sure you will be too.

—DR. JEFF DEGRAFF,
CO-AUTHOR OF *THE INNOVATION CODE* AND *THE CREATIVE MINDSET*

To meet Mo is to experience Mo! Thankfully, she's written a collection of stories so you too can experience Mo. *Pardon My Quirk* could easily be called, "The Wit and Wisdom from a Force of Nature." Mo's unique storytelling style balances irreverence with poignant, concise lessons whether your goal is to laugh, learn, think—or all three at once! If you're in need of a pick-me-up, you need this book.

—Jan R. Rutherford, Jr.,
Self-Reliant Leadership, LLC

Laugh? Check. Learn? Check again. Think? Yet another check. In *Pardon My Quirk*, the perpetually joyful Mo In addition to her kick-ass pilot creds, Mo Barrett is a compelling storyteller and inspirational speaker. In this book, she carefully compiles her best short and personal stories so that each chapter becomes a potential self-coaching tool and exercise in self-development. She promises to make you laugh, learn and think—I'd add tears of self-discovery to that—and she delivers in style!

—Helena Kim, PhD,
Author of *Soft Skills for Hard People*,
Coaching Psychologist

**I know what you're thinking and yes, they're real
...the thoughts that go through my head**

That was the working title of this book for the years I was considering writing it.

It was the working title when I signed the contract with the publisher.

It was the working title when I started working with an editor.

It was the working title until the night before the cover contest was over and my best friend suggested I could do better.

Sigh.

I was personally invested in, committed to and proud of my working title. I held on to that title for more than 10 years and was well in motion to be the final title.

As you might know, because you seem smart, the working title is not the final title.

So what happened?

My best friend was right.

I could do better.

And it helps to have a well-meaning friend by our side, reminding us that we can all do better.

So to those who make me better, thank you.

To my mom and dad for making me and making me push myself.

To Jen for finally noticing me after six months of grade A moves. I'm a better me when I'm with you.

To KatyKins for accepting that pivotal Boomer-in-a-Speedo airdrop. You make me a punnier creative (and you still owe me $860K).

To my siblings for spoiling me.

To my one-quarter, step-Japanese nieces for giving my faith in our future and continual pride in you both!

To Kymberlee for constantly up-leveling my work and reminding me about the power of story.

And to all of you making others better, thank you.

So on behalf of all those who make me do better, I present the book no longer titled, "I know what you're thinking and yes, they're real…the thoughts that go through my head."

There's More for Your Life at Sears

I'm at Sears, shopping for a socket wrench.

I look to the cash register and the lights in the store dim as a female cashier glows in the spotlight of a single beam from heaven. Through the chorus of singing cherubs, the cashier beckons me.

"Next in line!"

That's me!

Joy radiates from her small frame. Her gentle voice reveals an inner kindness to match her outer beauty.

Well-formed sentences in my brain crumble and a nonsensical series of syllables stumble out of my mouth.

The cashier stares at me with pity and confusion, patiently ringing up my purchase. Our transaction occurs wordlessly since vocabulary, my usual weapon of choice, fails me.

In an effort to redeem myself, and let's be honest, to see the lovely cashier once again, I go back the next day. I grab a tool I already have and wait in line for the same heaven-sent cashier.

Despite the arsenal of witty conversation starters I have prepared, vowels and consonants once again fail to fall in line and therefore fail to land wooingly onto the cashier's ears.

Another silent transaction and I'm headed home with a tool I don't need.

Days 3 and 4 follow the same format of great thoughts thwarted by failed execution.

Day 5, yet another unnecessary tool in hand, I reach the cashier.

This time, four days' worth of clever conversation are culled together and with my eloquence, I successfully invite this lovely cashier, whose name tag says "May," on a date.

This is how my dad answers my question, "How did you and Mom meet?"

Each time he tells the story, it gets more and more dramatic, and I swear strolling minstrels will be involved in the next version of it, so I stop asking him.

I turn to hear Mom's version, "Mom, how did you and Dad meet?"

Yawning, Mom rolls her eyes in an attempt to recall what seems to be a forgettable event. "I was working as a cashier at Sears in the tool department."

Ok, so far her story lines up with Dad's.

"This guy came up and had just one item and I rang him up."

Ok, still sounds the same. No mention of earth-shattering chatter, but missing are the dimmed lights and spotlight from above.

"Then, the next day, he came back for another tool." Another yawn from Mom, exhausted by the memory of these weary interactions so many years earlier.

"And then the next day he was back" says Mom, on the verge of falling asleep while telling her own story.

Mom continues wearily, "I think he came by every. single. day for about five days in a row, never saying anything, just buying one tool at a time. Then on that last day, he asked if I wanted to have lunch."

Mom punctuates the ending of her story with a shrug.

Each time Mom tells her version of their meeting, it gets more and more underwhelming to the point that I'm surprised they ever ended up together.

Of course, I'm grateful they did, because, well, I probably wouldn't be here if it weren't for the matchmaking services of the Sears tool department.

And since I <u>am</u> here, it's funny to compare the evolutions of the slogans for Sears to my own evolution:

- "Sears has everything"
- "There's more for your life at Sears"
- "Making moments matter"

They ring true for me because *Sears had everything* my dad needed *for his life*. And, the vastly different accounts of that five-day *moment that mattered* helps me realize that the same event can be analyzed from multiple viewpoints.

Just because the sound of silence is deafening in one version doesn't necessarily silence the singing cherubs in another version.

Those varying accounts of the same situation bring a valuable diversity to our lives. At least they did for the couple who would become Mr. and Mrs. Barrett, aka Mom and Dad.

> What's an event you and someone else
> saw from different perspectives?

My Mom FOIA'ed the DMV

What my mom lacks in romanticized storytelling abilities, she more than makes up for in her expressions of gratitude.

You've heard the argument about nature versus nurture, right? Nature pointing to those traits pre-wired in us, influenced by genetic inheritance and other biological factors. Nurture being products of our exposure to external factors, experience and learning. One thing I always figured belonged in the nurture category was gratitude.

As far as I know, scientists have yet to discover the genome for gratefulness in the genetic blueprint for our species, but one thing we can be pretty sure of is that the blueprint for happiness includes gratitude. Multitudes of studies have shown that gratitude has emotional, personal, health, career and social advantages, all of which lead to increased happiness. And we can learn to be grateful from being around people who are thankful.

In other words, we can be nurtured by other people who model gratitude.

Recently, I came across a familial artifact that might reveal a little more nature than nurture when it comes to gratitude. Filed under M (for miscellaneous), I found a letter where my mom had FOIA'ed the DMV. I know that's a lot of letters, but my predilection for acronyms is equal parts nature and nurture.

My mom had sent a letter to the Department of Motor Vehicles invoking the Freedom of Information Act, which requires disclosure of unreleased information controlled by the U.S. government upon request.

Quick background in American law: FOIA is rooted in a desire for accountability through transparency "to ensure an informed citizenry, vital to the functioning of a democratic society, needed to check against corruption and to hold the governors accountable to the governed." So sayeth the Department of Justice.

However, corruption and accountability were not at the root of my mom's request. My mom FOIA'ed the DMV in order to identify the "tall, young white male driver of a white, four-door sedan with Virginia license plate number XXXX-XXX" (you can FOIA me if you're interested in the actual license plate number).

Mom's letter goes into exhaustive detail about an interaction a few days earlier at a grocery store. The yet-to-be-identified tall young man bought my dad, a veteran, a magazine about World War II after their conversation about the war while waiting for a price check (or someone paying by check).

This letter was written *after* my mom had already gone back to the grocery store and tracked down the cashier to see if she knew the shopper. And I wouldn't put it past my mom to have surveilled the store to wait for the tall young man to return to the scene of the gift. Some call it casing the joint or stalking; Mom calls it gratitude.

And somewhere out there is a tall young man, hopefully no longer driving the same white four-door sedan, who probably has no idea the impact his seemingly small gesture made on my mom, my dad and me.

As a veteran, my dad felt seen and appreciated—a privilege not all veterans have experienced.

As a veteran's wife, my mom saw her pride reflected in this man's gift.

As a daughter, I saw how the benefactor's actions affected my parents. And Mom's letter models the lengths to which we can go to express our gratitude.

I may have some gratitude DNA coursing through my genes, but we can all nurture each other to notice the good deeds around us.

Also coursing through my genes are index cards (I have a genetic predisposition to office supplies) so when I don't have time to FOIA state agencies, I can at least jot a personalized note of thanks for an act that made an impact on me.

Frugality is also a biological inheritance so, naturally, I love that gratitude is free. It costs us only the time to notice and acknowledge. That's an investment in my overall happiness that I can get behind.

> Choose one person who's made an impact on you and thank them with something more than just words.

M Is for Miscellaneous

I found that letter where Mom FOIA'ed the DMV in one of many Rolodex files in my childhood home. For those of you unfamiliar with Rolodexes, it's an old-school paper filing system typically for addresses. Rolodex is actually a portmanteau for rolling index, because the specially notched cards snapped into a rotating spindle with alphabetized dividers (unless you fiddled with the divider tabs and put *I* before *E*, you rebel).

For those of you unfamiliar with portmanteaus, come geek out with me over etymology sometime.

For those of you unfamiliar with etymology, come hang out and…you know what? Stop distracting me! Where was I? Oh yeah, the Rolodex.

I find a card with the combination to the firesafe. Correction, I find cards (plural) with the combination to the firesafe.

It's under *C*, presumably for "combination."

It's under *I*, I think because it was a piece of "information."

It's under *L*, obviously for "lock."

It's under *S*, for "safe."

And then, it's under *M* for "miscellaneous."

M could have its own Rolodex because my dad filed everything under Miscellaneous. We used to make fun of my dad about that, but now that I've tried sev-er-al ways to organize my files, I understand. Filing stuff is easy…if you don't ever plan on referencing the stuff you file. But if that's the case, I'm not sure why you're filing anything in the first place. It seems to me that the crucial element of a filing system is to make your life easier when you need to retrieve the information.

I read books and articles and Wikipedia how-tos on "the best" filing system. I watch YouTube videos and interviews with professional organizers. I talk to and mirror the systems of others who seem to have their collective shyte together. Years of reading, watching, talking, stalking and filing has taught me that the best filing system is my filing system. And the best filing system for you is your filing system.

The way you file info needs to align with the way your brain categorizes data. Forcing our paperwork into someone else's folders may not suffice when it's time to recall that information (and if you literally filed it in someone else's folders, it may not be conveniently located near you).

Outside the filing cabinet, I've caught myself trying to fit into someone else's mold (not the fungus…although I am a fun-gal). Whether it was the way I studied, the way I lead or the way I filed, the most successful, the most natural and the most reliable method was the way that made sense to me.

Whether it's the way you parent, lead or file, find a system that works for you. And if you're like Dad and me, that may involve intense cross-categorization. But I'd rather have the information stored in multiple places rather than not at all.

And with a combination like that, I know I'm safe.

What's a task you do differently than "most" other people?

Carl's Puerto Rican

Regardless of where Dad filed stuff, he did so unapologetically. He consistently used the system that worked for him. He knew who he was and how he was wired.

There's a lot to be said for knowing who you are.

It's an idyllic spring afternoon in Northern Virginia. The weather's transformation from gray and cold mirrors the personality changes happening in the National Capital Region. Optimism and hope bloom like the cherry blossoms, renewing our resolve to cut through the red tape entangling the federal government.

It's also a day to witness a fellow Air Force officer vow to love, honor and obey his girlfriend. I am part of the traditional military arch of sabers under which the newlywed couple exits the church. I'm in the arch contingent because the Air Force officer who has just said "I do" is an office mate of my new girlfriend, Jen.

And now we are on the perfectly manicured lawn of Mount Vernon, the home of our nation's first president, George Washington. We're in our most formal Air Force uniform, the tuxedo equivalent: high heels, long-slitted skirt, tuxedo shirt and jacket, cufflinks, cummerbund and petite decorative medals on our chest (her medals are on her chest, mine are on mine).

No one can hear the gentle clink of the miniature military medals because joyous conversations chirp around us in small flocks of gathered friends and family. The arch team are all officemates of Jen, so I'm a bit of an outsider. Together we all appear as outsiders because the eight of us are the only uniformed attendees. We look more like catering staff than rice-throwers. And even though I'm dressed like the other seven, I am more of an outsider than the other seven.

The military's Don't Ask, Don't Tell policy is 13 years old, and most military members have adopted the Live and Let Live policy. Officially, Jen and I are roommates with the fiscal good sense to combine our housing allowances to afford decent living quarters. It doesn't require top secret interrogative insight to infer that we are literally "roommates," in that we sleep in the same room (and bed).

The perfectly coiffed lawn of George Washington's home isn't the place for the revelation of relationship definition accuracy, so I'm happy to play the part of "Jen's friend." I am also happy to be "Jen's friend" at the high-dollar wedding reception with an open bar of top-shelf products.

Not wanting the products to spoil, Jen's office mate Carl asks Jen to be his plus one to retrieve beverages to quench the thirst and sobriety of the saber team. Jen enthusiastically jumps at the opportunity. Hidden by her introverted exterior is an attraction to Carl. His name frequently comes up in our Pentagon job debriefs each evening. I suspect the attraction is a professional one, because, well, Carl is married. Oh, and Jen's gay (not that you asked, but don't tell).

I engage in small talk with the rest of the team while we wait for our alcohol couriers. My eye detects a fast-moving target in an otherwise peaceful cadence of movement.

It's Jen.

No longer a two-ship formation with Carl, she is now solo, laden with a full tray of drinks. She is sprinting across the lawn, her miniature medals fluttering with her gait, her high heels denied the time to stab and sink into the soft ground.

She gets to our table, leaving Carl confused and alone at the bar.

Breathlessly, excitedly, she pants, "Guess what?!"

I have zero guesses. Jen gives me zero seconds to come up with one.

"CARL'S. PUERTO. RICAN!"

I'm not sure why Carl's ethnicity is the most important drink quest discovery.

"I don't understand," I stall as I try to tie together discordant pieces so I can catch up to this conversation.

Jen offers her explanation, "Carl's Puerto Rican too!"

Ah yes, super helpful.

Those three additional letters, well, two actually, provide insight.

While getting drinks and revealing his ethnicity, Carl had given Jen a cultural connection. She finally found a natural propellant to rocket their work relationship into a friendship.

But my relationship with Jen is also beginning to take off as we establish our own balance. So this is a pivotal moment. I can share in her ethnic connection excitement, or I can choose launch-blocking honesty.

I choose honesty.

"That's great, babe, but you're not Puerto Rican...you're Portuguese."

Jen nearly drops the tray of drinks, her face broadcasting the cumulative emotion of learning about Santa, the Easter Bunny, gravity and the Tooth Fairy all at the same time.

But it reminds me just how important connection is, even for a strong introvert. Jen's desire to in some way, *any* way, be connected to Carl resulted in her jumping to a cultural conclusion after only the letter *P* came out of Carl's mouth.

Social connections are as important to our survival and flourishing as the need for food, safety, shelter and an open bar. Seek out those things that bind us together, even if it's only a story about being ethnically connected.

What's a special connection you found you had with someone?

Japanese Drag Queen

One thing that connects me to many of my friends is female barbershop singing. Unlike some "barbershop brats" who were born with a pitch pipe in their mouths, I didn't discover barbershop until late in life. And thank God I did.

There is something so welcoming, energizing, supportive and addicting about the "cult" of barbershoppers. While there are many barbershop organizations, I joined the collective known as Sweet Adelines International. These female a cappella singers remain the most positive and encouraging group I have ever been a part of. As a Type A competitor, the fact that most Sweet Adeline choruses attend competitions was icing atop an already sweet treat.

Sweet Adeline performers get judged or graded in four different categories: sound, music, expression and showmanship. The first three categories focus on the production of the song—how well the singers individually and collectively sing, tune, interpret, dictate, emote, arrange finesse, communicate and deliver the lyrical story.

That fourth category, though…that's the focus for today.

Showmanship is an evaluation of the ensemble's command of the stage, their characterization and energy during the performance and how unified their visual presentation is. Within the showmanship category is "makeup and grooming."

Because barbershop is a team sport, individual makeup application is done to create one complete chorus look and NOT to spotlight any one individual performer. And with that, the purpose of the makeup is to define facial features so the audience and the judges can see the subtle facial expressions of communication during story singing.

And because our facial expressions are subtle and because the audience and judges are a fair distance away and *because* we sing under bright stage lights, the individual performer has to increase the vibrancy and intensity of stage makeup.

Translation: archaeologists could dig through the depths of makeup caked on our faces.

I'm at the regional competition with my chorus, in the middle of stage prep, which means I am slathering on makeup like a mason buttering a wall with mortar.

Brown paste that's supposed to be the base layer.

Red stuff just for my cheeks.

Purple powder on top of my eyelids.

A pencil for my eyes that is always nearly the scribe for a story where I blind myself with it.

It may not be difficult to discern, but I'm about as familiar with makeup application as I am with bricklaying.

You may not be able to tell from my photo on the back of this book in your hands (don't look now), but I am not the girly-girl makeup type. So to compensate for my lack of cosmetic prowess, a makeup chaperone hovers over my shoulder, making sure I have enough makeup on and that I match the layers upon layers of product on her face.

I'm almost done applying the paint and spackle to my face when my phone rings. With my makeup trowel in one hand and a vat of mortar in the other, I use a random knuckle to accept the call on speakerphone. It's my friend Beth from high school who's coming to watch us compete. She's calling to ask if she'll be able to find me on stage.

It's a fair question since we haven't seen each other in person in a looooong time, and I would be dressed identically to the woman next to me on stage…and the woman next to her…and the woman next to…you get it. Basically 70 women all wearing the same thing.

I start describing where I'll be standing when the chorus is on stage. I quickly realize I'm screwing up the stage lefts and rights and audience member stage lefts and rights, which I think are just lefts and rights.

So, I need to visualize what Beth will see from the audience.

I look up at the mirror.

Ho-ly vampire, batman!

In the mirror, I don't see my reflection.

Let me rephrase: I don't see me in the reflection.

What I see in the mirror is someone who has overdone it with makeup (think Glamour Shots meets P. T. Barnum).

Lefts and rights no longer matter because I have a faster way for Beth to find me. I tell her what to look for by telling her precisely what I see in the mirror.

"Uhhhhhh, just look for the Japanese drag queen."

I certainly mean no offense to the Japanese (I am half Japanese) or to drag queens (I wish I could look that beautiful). It's just an honest assessment of what I look like, and it serves the purpose of telling Beth how to find me.

"Oh come on, I know you're gonna look gorgeous."

"Beth, thank you, but I'm telling you, if you want to find me on the stage, just look for the Japanese drag queen."

Fast-forward to after the competition. I find Beth and we catch up on life. And then, the question I really need answered, "So, were you able to find me on stage?"

"Yea."

"And, how did you find me?"

Beth quietly and sheepishly responds, "Japanese drag queen."

I didn't get hung up on my Japanese drag queen appearance because how I look as an individual is how I need to look in order to complement the chorus unit appearance. And there is more to me than just my appearance. My real contribution is my singing voice, the notes I offer to complement the notes being sung by the rest of the chorus, the notes that complete our chords.

Many times, we get caught up in our appearance, labels and external identifiers and lose sight of the fact that we are more than those superficial labels and identifiers. We all have a powerful contribution to offer, our own notes to complete the chords with the notes from others around us.

So, no matter how much mortar you trowel on your face, reflect on the fact that your makeup is determined by who you are inside, not how you appear on the outside.

What contributions do you make that
help you complete the "chords" around
you?

Your Other Pilot Is a Woman!

One thing that's hard to tell about me just by visual reconnaissance is that I'm a pilot (unless I'm in the cockpit of a plane and it's flying, then that's a fairly strong indicator that I might be a pilot).

My very first operational flying assignment in the Air Force is to a small squadron in Central America. Panama to be exact. It's a tight-knit unit of all men, and I move to Panama with some trepidation about being the first and only "chick stick" in the squadron. It turns out to be an unfounded apprehension as the boys' club welcomes me with open arms (wings?) because, as a unit of professionals, all they really care about is whether you're a good pilot.

Our crews of three fly missions throughout Central and South America on one of the 10 C-27 aircraft stationed there. The C-27 is an Italian-made twin engine turboprop aircraft specializing in short-field takeoffs and landings. The majority of the fields we fly into are small dirt strips tucked in the valleys of the Andes Mountains or along the banks of the Amazon River.

Finding the field is more often than not a visual hunt, aided by unofficially navigating to the AM radio station closest to the airfield. Once the hopefully correct radio station is tuned in, it becomes the soundtrack for our approach above the triple canopy jungle, while blue and yellow macaws fly off our wing in formation. Assuming the macaw escorts and AM signal bring us to the right airfield, the next phase of flight includes a pass over the runway without landing.

There are two reasons for this.

Firstly, to cross-check what's beneath us against the information we were given in the pre-brief. A lot of the villages we fly into are only accessible by air, so making sure we are about to land at the right one is crucial. The second reason we fly over the runway once before landing is to announce our arrival. By announce, I mean scare, because the arrival message is intended for the donkeys, horses and other random four-legged beasts grazing on or milling about the landing strip. The second pass usually ends with the landing (unless a brazen four-legged takes the field again) and then we do an impressive short-field landing, enabled by max braking and throwing our two engines into reverse.

Far from my first sortie in the C-27, I end up as the copilot on the crew flying the first U.S. aircraft to an airfield in Tena, a small city in central Ecuador, right in the heart of the Amazon Rainforest.

Our macaws and radio broadcast bring us to the correct field, and on our first pass, we are pleased to see no four-legged creatures fighting us for use of the runway. Our first pass <u>does</u> reveal what appears to be the entire village population lining the airfield perimeter, peering through the chain-link fence. I suspect that none of the corrugated tin-roofed buildings surrounding the field are occupied, as it seems that the first U.S. aircraft landing in Tena warrants time off from work and school and anything else going on in the town.

We put on a good show and create an impressive dirt cloud with our engines and brakes. Our landing roll out is so truncated that we are able to turn into the mid-strip parking apron without having to back taxi.

As we turn onto the parking apron, I see the best-dressed marshaller I have ever seen. His wide smile is a better guide than any marshaling wand I've ever followed. As we start getting closer to him, his welcoming face rapidly deteriorates into concern, surprise and fear. His visual instructions about where to park have frantically disintegrated into a "stop here and NOW!" frenzy of arm movements that transcend any language barrier.

It is very clear that he sees something that's disconcertingly awry that must be addressed immediately.

Now I'm concerned that we have an engine fire or have blown a corrugated tin roof off a building or, worse, that we've blown over a villager. Or that an engine fire has melted a corrugated tin roof <u>onto</u> a villager.

My aircraft commander rapidly transfers control of the aircraft to me and gets out of his seat while I shut down the left engine. As the turboprop blades slow and stop to no longer be a decapitation threat, my aircraft commander runs to the marshaller.

I sit ready, refreshing my mind on where the egress points and fire extinguishers are. I watch my commander and the marshaller and realize my Spanish would not have been adequate to get us through the conversation, although I do know that "*fuego*" would have meant "get the fire extinguisher."

My commander eventually gets our host to stop waving and pointing at our aircraft, then pats the shoulder of the now-much-calmer Ecuadorian marshaller. I translate this as there is no engine fire, all roofs are still in position and no villagers have been harmed by our arrival.

My commander gets back into his cockpit seat, welcomed only by my impatient interrogation, "What was that about? What did he say?"

As it turns out, the conversation had been in English... and had been one-sided.

The information our marshaller was so frantic to relay, was, "CAPTAIN! Your other pilot. It is a woman!"

For the best-dressed marshaller in Ecuador, "pilot" and "male pilot" are the same, and there has been no scenario in his life where "female" preceded "pilot."

So our landing wasn't only a first for Tena, Ecuador—it was also a first for him.

What paradigms have you shifted or broken?

Un Beso Fuerte

Not long after the mayor of Tena, Ecuador learns that girls could fly, I find myself as the copilot for an orientation flight of 22 male Panamanian civic leaders.

Our crew stands in a line outside the plane, greeting each gentleman as he boards. Our male loadmaster gets a powerful handshake from each civic leader, as does our male aircraft commander. I, however, simply get a delicate kiss on each cheek as their presumed flight attendant, or in this day and age, "stewardess."

We follow them on board, the two pilots taking a left turn into the cockpit and the loadmaster taking a right turn into the cargo and passenger area. We all get on our headsets and start running checklists. The other pilot and I get the engines spinning while the loadmaster briefs our passengers on standard procedures and safety instructions.

Through my headset, I hear the loadmaster call to us, "Uhmmmmm, these guys are really freaked out back here. They're not listening to a word of my brief. They're just staring up front at the cockpit." It seems a woman in the cockpit is a new sight for these Panamanian men and is not a sight that makes them comfortable.

We take off uneventfully and get up to our cruise altitude with the autopilot engaged. The aircraft commander, well-versed in handling Latin machismo, transfers autopilot-watching duties to me and leaves the cockpit.

Over the headset, the loadmaster provides me a play-by-play as our aircraft commander takes his sweet time to slowly greet each and every Panamanian civic leader on board, none of whom take their concerned eyes off the cockpit, knowing I am the only one up there.

Hopefully, it's not a surprise that we make it safely home after a couple hours in the air. As the civic leaders deplane, the loadmaster and the other pilot get zero attention. Instead, I get all the attention as each Panamanian man gives me *un beso fuerte* and an awkwardly long hug immediately after stepping off the aircraft.

They may have boarded the plane thinking women couldn't (or shouldn't) fly. But they left knowing that at least *they* had survived a flight with a woman at the controls. I was happy to facilitate that "first" for them and to show them that even a woman could competently fly a plane.

Of course, all I had to do to prove my professional competence was not crash the plane. The bar isn't always high.

So when we run into misperceptions or inaccuracies about us, take the time to see and seize the opportunity to provide a new reality, even if it's by just not crashing.

How has being a "first" or "only" made you feel?

The Loudest Voice We Hear

My crash-in with the Panamanian civic leaders wasn't the first time someone underestimated me. As a matter of fact, my most influential underestimation happened in high school and almost kept me from going to the Air Force Academy.

It's the middle of a school day. My friend and I are wandering the halls of our high school. Neither one of us are typically the type to skip class, but it *is* nearing the end of our junior year so we *are* one year closer to ruling the school. Sixteen years of obedience training have me on high alert as a high school authority figure rounds the corner. We quickly evade into the nearest legitimate foxhole...the career center.

An adult in an all-white military uniform is getting ready to push a videotape into the VCR. The flotilla of "Go Navy" propaganda floating around the career center advertises the fact that it's Naval Academy recruitment day. My knowledge of the Naval Academy is limited to the fact that my friend's dad graduated from there. But since the aggressors in the hallway outside the career center threaten my goodie-two-shoes reputation, I feel compelled to remain hostage to the Naval Academy recruiter.

He pushes play on his brainwash video. Nothing happens.

He queues up the video of the Army's version of the Naval Academy to pinpoint if the trouble is with the video or the video player. West Point fails too.

As a last resort, he tries the Air Force Academy video, since their school is "just like the others."

The Air Force Academy video actually works and it is nothing like anything I have seen before. Up until this moment, my life plan has included following in my dad's and my brother's footsteps to the Air Force via the same path my brother took: ROTC at Virginia Tech.

The thought of attending Seasick University or Hudson High has never crossed my mind, but that Air Force school? Now I want that.

Before the graduating Air Force Academy cadets can even ceremoniously throw their caps into the air, I am en route to my guidance counselor's office. A visit to see him will both legitimize my time out of the classroom and give me the opportunity to tell him I am going to apply to the Air Force Academy.

I burst into his office and tell him my plan. My guidance counselor, cleverly disguised as the head football coach, laughs. He counsels me, "Miss Barrett. Your grades aren't good enough. Your standardized test scores aren't high enough. Community college is a more realistic goal for you." He cannot be more cavalier or patronizing.

My newly hatched college dream of the Academy resonates with me more loudly than his condescension and more strongly than his letterman jacket–wearing football jocks. It is an inexplicable magnetic pull more powerful than my compliance to this grown-up's advice, an adult whose very task, according to the sign on his office door, is to guide and counsel me on my future.

I remember that this is *my* future, *my* goal and so therefore, *my* decision.

I start the lengthy process of applying to my new, first-choice school. Congressional nominations, interviews, essays, forms in quadruplicate, medical evaluations and physical fitness tests. Finally, the day arrives when I get to prove that my high school guidance counselor is absolutely…right.

My grades aren't good enough, my test scores aren't high enough and soon after high school, I am, in fact, enrolled at the safety school my guidance counselor predicted. I wallow in self-pity as a failed college applicant relegated to living with her parents and attending the local community college.

Since I have the same address I've had all my life, it isn't difficult for a flyer to find its way to me in the mail. It's an opportunity to apply for a six-month service academy preparatory school. The flyer brags an 83% success rate of getting its graduates into the service academies.

By this time, I've already secured a spot at another college, more prestigious than the safety of community college but certainly not an institution with the allure of The United States Air Force Academy.

Do I abandon my newly discovered dream of being an Air Force Academy cadet and press on with the life waiting for me at a normal college, underage drinking at college parties interspersed with optional attendance at the classes in a lighter academic load?

Or do I take this preparatory school up on its offer, a "gap" year with a singular focus of getting me and other persistent kids into a military service academy, with the reward of that year being four years of a rigidly controlled life while carrying a 21-hour academic semester load?

My sister, Barb, sees the flyer with its promised opportunity lying on the kitchen table. Casually, she comments, "If they'd accepted women at the academies when I went to college, I would have done anything to apply."

One casual comment from someone I admire nullifies any question I have and makes very clear the only logical choice. I relinquish the commitment to the "normal" school and launch Operation Gap Year. Six months later, I reapply to the Air Force Academy and become part of the 83% success rate.

Once we choose a goal or a path, the only way a naysayer has power over the outcome is if we give it to them. We may or may not ever realize that people are listening and weighing what we say and could very well be influenced by our inputs.

People are listening, so make sure the counsel we provide is uplifting and encouraging. And as we listen to others, make sure the loudest voice we hear is the one that speaks from our heart.

What's something you've accomplished
after someone said you couldn't?

Four Years?

Sometimes, in tuning out the naysayers in order to listen to our own voice, we miss a group humming along blissfully out of tune.

As an Air Force Academy cadet, I remain grounded in my hometown roots, especially to the church where I was baptized and confirmed, the church where I have grown up. This crew has been part of my flight from childhood onward. They have watched me target goals, crash and burn, reattack and finally achieve my objectives.

I write monthly letters to the church, which are reprinted in the newsletter and posted on the bulletin board. My messages navigate them through the daily activities of normal college life: sailing in gliders, classes in aeronautics, flying solo in single-engine planes, et cetera.

Located 10 miles west of Washington, DC, our congregation is heavily armed with those employed by the military industry. Every service academy is represented by its alumni who are currently serving a

Pentagon sentence or have stayed in the area after the parole of retirement.

It's the middle of my junior year, and I'm milling around the fellowship hall after the Sunday service. The sugary sweet scent of cookies and lemonade is cut by an overdose of cologne and perfume. The fragrance of freshly brewed coffee soars through the hall, weakening the resulting assault of coffee breath.

A sharp bouquet of "eau de old lady" pre-announces the arrival of one of the more senior ladies of our church.

She gently asks, "How's your training going?" Her over-aspirated *H* transports eye-watering breath.

"Fine, ma'am, thank you for asking." My practiced military bearing provides a steady defense against the nasal assault.

"How much longer do you have dear?"

Silently, I pray, "*Dear God, exorcise her demon breath.*"

"Two years, ma'am."

Her face wrinkles into what looks like disgust, making me wonder if my silent prayer was indeed silent. I quickly recategorize the look as one of confusion. She inches closer as if physical distance reduction will bring clarity.

"Hhhhhuh. How long have you been there?" Her *H* habit hampers hope of handling her halitosis.

"Two years." Brevity is my friend.

"How long is the school?" *H*'s are hers.

I don't mean to flaunt my mathematical prowess, but I have already told her I've been there two years and have two left. I go ahead and do the math and relay that this is a four-year program.

She reels back (prayer answered) in astonishment, shouting, "FOUR YEARS? To become a STEWARDESS?"

It's my turn to over-aspirate as I reset my patience with a long sigh before clearing up the confusion that the United States Air Force Academy is not in the business of producing flight attendants.

My brief edification that the Academy is a four-year bachelor of science degree-awarding institution followed by at least six years of military service is a good reminder that some people support us even though they don't really understand what it is we're aiming for.

There are people who doubt us without knowing what we're capable of doing. The more important reminder is to persevere despite anyone's lack of clarity or disbelief.

In the end, these are our goals. No one else's. Choose them, believe in them, pursue them and believe in yourself. That's what matters. That, and knowing where the emergency exits are located.

What goal are you pursuing, despite others not fully understanding what you're doing?

Strum-Strum-Sticker

Perseverance toward our goals and withstanding those who might not understand or encourage us can be exhausting. And there are days when our own resolve falters.

My best friend, Katy, has wanted a new ukulele for about a year now. She talks about it, knows the specific one she wants and has multiple screenshots of it. After a year of hearing her pine for it without purchasing it, she seems to be just stringing herself along.

When I ask her what's stopping her from buying it, she says she wants to "earn" it. When I ask her what would make her feel like she's earned it, she says more consistency playing her current uke. When I ask her what's stopping her from more consistent playing of her current uke, the line goes silent.

Soon thereafter, I get a texted photo of her 30-days-to-a-new-uke calendar. It's a simple 30-day hand-drawn calendar, the last day of which says, "YOU DID IT!"

To accompany her calendar, she has a roll of stickers typically reserved for her younger piano students. Each day she practices her ukulele, she rewards herself with a sticker.

Via photo updates, I watch as the stickers strut their way onto the 30-days-to-a-new-uke calendar. Katy's photo updates are always upbeat and there's no fret that her new uke is within reach. At day 19, my photo update doesn't arrive at the typical time. As an invested subscriber to the 30-days-to-a-new-uke calendar, I am worried about the fate of the new uke.

"Did you get your sticker today?"

"Yea," Katy says with about as much enthusiasm as a kid about to start a mandatory chore of scrubbing toilets.

"What's up?"

"I just wasn't feeling it today. I taught lessons for nearly 11 hours, had to scurry around running errands after that and then had a three-hour rehearsal."

"Ok, but did you practice your ukulele?"

"Yea," said as if I hadn't heard it the first time.

"And your calendar got a sticker?"

"Yea, but it felt more like strum-strum-sticker." Her monotone "strum-strum-sticker" has a death-march cadence.

And despite the grim delivery of the strum-strum-sticker ballad, the bottom line is that she had practiced her ukulele, earned her sticker and was still on her way to her dream uke.

I've certainly had days that felt like "strum-strum-sticker," the days where I'm just not feeling it. Whether it's studying, working out or trying to stay on the nutritional reset known as Whole 30 (or, as I end up calling it, "Whole 10"), my "strum-strum-sticker" days are the ones where I don't really feel like I'm having any impact on my own goals or any impact whatsoever.

Katy's 30-days-to-a-new-uke calendar reminds me that sometimes we just have to power through and "strum-strum-sticker." Some days are more of a challenge than others, but I assure you there's a sticker on the other side of the struggle.

What reward system do you use as you drive toward a goal?

The Beauty of Art

Speaking of struggles, I have a slight propensity toward perfectionist tendencies. I have been known to chase down complete strangers in order to "fix" their backpack or bag zippers (the two zippers should always be together and centered on the bag and aligned with other zipper couples).

Ok, "slight" might be an understatement.

My dad always said there were two people you never wanted to hear say "oops": your hairdresser and your surgeon. And there certainly are some tasks where we should strive for perfection. Although I'm not sure zipper alignment has the teeth to rise to the level of haircutting and surgeoning.

So we're left with Vince Lombardi reminding us to chase an unattainable perfection in order to catch excellence. Otherwise, we can fall victim to the negative side of perfectionism: doubts, concerns and overwhelming pressure.

The last place I expect to be striving for perfection or excellence is on vacation in Greece, unless the skill I'm striving for is relaxation and mindlessness. So after a day of mindlessly relaxing, I'm perusing coasters in the quaint store of a local artisan.

Handmade, individually crafted coasters are stacked on the table in front of me. Having recently hiked to the town of Oia on the northwestern tip of Santorini, I am drawn to gorgeous, crisp, aqua-colored coasters mimicking the classic blue and white skyline of Greece. Painted in high-contrast silver on each coaster is a pair of fish.

Committed to buying this coaster, I also realize I can't have just one (thank you, Lay's potato chips). I sort through the stack, looking for a match. Undeterred by the amount of coasters I have to look through, I am rewarded with a coaster identical to the one I have already picked out. A perfect pair!

Thrilled by the hunt and motivated by the challenge, I seek out a third coaster to match the pair. Soon, I have it! I hold in my hands a trio of coasters where all six fish are oriented in the same direction, their bright silver coats popping vibrantly, and identically, from the rich blue background.

In a textbook exhibition of compulsive buying disorder, I frantically forage through the yet un-foraged coasters, looking for "just one more" to round out my set. Ironically, or coincidentally, compulsive buying disorder is also known as *oniomania*, which is rooted in the Greek language. The word is made up of "sale" and "insanity," but obviously it's lost something in translation because I can stop anytime I want. Which will be after I find this fourth coaster. Maybe.

The artist comes over to see what this insane American is looking for. I show him my perfect pair (plus one). I enlist his help in looking for the last piece of his handiwork to square off my set.

Together we sift through coasters and with his undiscerning eye he chooses coasters with off-centered fish, lackluster silver painted fish and even a coaster with THREE FISH! In critiquing his selections, I realize I'm also criticizing his artistry. But instead of taking offense, he takes pride in the things I'm pointing out.

He laughs and with a twinkle in his eye says, "The beauty of art is in its imperfection."

Damn.

Drop coaster.

There is so much truth and power in his simple statement.

I grab a fourth coaster (it has two fish at least…I'm not a monster) and pay my imperfection mentor.

Now I have a set of four imperfectly matched coasters to remind me that perfect is the enemy of good.

I try to see the beauty in life's imperfections but I still struggle. I do try to leave strangers' backpack zippers alone, for the most part. What can I say? I'm an imperfect work in progresss.

> Name a time you drove yourself insane seeking perfection when there was a beautiful "good" already there.

Pull Your Head Out

My most prolific zipper-fixing seems to happen at airports. But since I'm trying to refrain from imposing my perfectionism on others, today, I'm sitting by the airport restrooms. Don't judge me; there's some good people watching to be had there.

At the airport, there's a restroom for the men on the left and for the ladies on the right. A male traveler, preoccupied with the organic light-emitting diode technology of his cell phone, absentmindedly walks into...the ladies' room. A female traveler, seeing the man do this, chooses the opposite restroom, which she presumes is <u>not</u> the men's room, but it is.

The woman wastes no time figuring out her mistake, immediately coming back out of the men's room. But before she can roll into the correct restroom, another man sees a woman come out of the door on the left and assumes that must be the ladies' room, so he chooses the right door, which ironically is the wrong door.

The woman, having seen the wall-mounted toilets in the "women's" room but then seeing two men go into the "right" room—as in, on the right—looks very confused and flees the scene.

In the end, I watch no fewer than four men go into the ladies' room and three ladies go into the men's room before the next contestant in "toilet or urinal" verifies restroom accuracy by cross-checking the label on the door.

Have you ever caught yourself on autopilot, living life with your head down, following the lead of others, stuck in habitual patterns?

We get in trouble when we stop thinking for ourselves. That's right, I said it. When you stop thinking for yourself, you're in trouble.

When I catch myself living like this, I can hear my pilot training instructor yelling at me, "Barrett, pull your head out!" His words leak from my memory into the pipes of my daily life, flushing me off of the throne of just following the crowd.

We can all benefit from that advice. Pull your head out, keep your head up and be sure you're aiming for the right door.

What's your motto to remind you to pay attention?

No-Fly Zone

If you don't have the luxury of people watching at an airport bathroom, might I suggest your own living room?

It's a crisp autumn day, cool enough for a sweater but warm enough for open windows, which is precisely how my living room is outfitted. The door to the back patio is also open, as are the windows in the kitchen. The smell of freshly cut grass glides in on the crisp fall breeze. Secretly, I invite a colorful leaf to flutter in. It's exactly what I would expect to come in and augment this tranquil scene.

What I do <u>not</u> expect is a gigantic housefly, which is what does invade my living room of tranquility. This bastard jets in, diving toward my head, circling around me like I'm some sort of air traffic control tower. The directions I am giving to the noncompliant beast in the pattern are pretty clear, and they are, "Get. Out."

He appears to want to get out as much as I want him to get out, because from the moment he invites himself into my living room, his flight path is erratic. His trans–living room flight is interrupted by…a wall, which he crashes into, stunning himself. Serves him right. This was literally a no-fly zone until his rude interruption.

I watch him fly around the living room, buzzing into one wall, then another, then the ceiling, then into the lampshade, the TV and yet another wall. I know this makes it seem like I have a huge living room. I do not.

This fly is just so frantic that he covers a lot of area in a short flight. I feel helpless because the fly and I want the same thing—his departure—but chasing him and trying to shoo him out with a newspaper seems like it would send mixed messages, especially because I read the newspaper on my iPad.

I apologize for using the male pronoun, but as the fly never once stopped to ask for directions, I have to assume…

I sit idly on my couch, watching the fly's airshow. The only win-win outcome I can hope for is that the fly will depart the area via one of the several openings to the outside. While waiting for that to happen, my peripheral vision picks up graceful movements near the open window. A dainty dandelion poof gently hugs the autumn breeze, riding it in through the window, coasting into my living room.

I watch as the poof floats effortlessly through the room. The poof catches the cross breeze from the patio door opening, allowing itself to be quietly coaxed in a different direction. Hypnotically, the myriad mini jet streams propel and nudge the poof, its calm soar mesmerizing. The relaxed vibe of the poof radiates toward me, stopping time long enough for me to breathe deeply, align my Chaka Khan, salute the sun and stare downwardly at my dog (this joke slays in California).

Soon, the dandelion poof slips the surly bonds of my living room, joining the tumbling mirth of sun-split clouds outside my home.

I look back at the still-chaotic flight path of the damn fly, still banging into walls, still unable to find his way out, outwitted by the brainless poof of a WEED.

I sit back on my couch.

I think.

Wow, I have a lot of spare time.

Honestly, in a day and age when my attention span is sourced from a shrinking stockpile, I'm impressed at the sustainability of my focus.

I know I've logged time as that fly. Frantically buzzing around in situations, trying to navigate in a new environment, banging my head against walls and ceilings (and lampshades and TVs). Those times leave me feeling unprepared or anxious, with the anxiety usually a result of being unprepared. These are the times when I fail to stop, ask for or get help.

But there have been times when I'm able to get a break, catch my breath and float on the currents of life like the poof of a dandelion, without a care in the world. Those are the moments that bring me respite for any future frantic flights. Taking the time to just drift on the current for a moment helps me regroup. I have to let life gently coax and nudge me one way or another until I find myself on the jet stream to guide me on laughter-silvered wings to my next success.

There are times to be like the frantic fly, but taking on the personality of a poof makes it possible to be present in the now, hypersensitive to the world around us. Concentrating our energy on the task at hand allows us to act deliberately, not reactively. Methodical focus during the planning phase equips us to handle future pop-up issues more effectively and quickly.

The poof may be the brainless wing of a weed, but we'd fly onto our next success more quickly if we took the time to float first. Sometimes we have to slow down now to speed up later.

Name a time when slowing down helped you speed up.

Purple Dragon

One thing that slowing down has allowed me to do is reflect. Let's jump back to the days of my youth. Ah, my youth. If only I had realized how fast it would swim by.

It's summertime in Northern Virginia. At five years old, I'm too young to realize that summer means no school. To me, summer means trips to the pool with my siblings. As the youngest of six, there's a rotation of siblings I get to go to the pool with. Today, it's with my sister, Jan, and brother, Earl.

We walk hand in hand the short distance to the community pool. The smell of the hot asphalt makes me glad I'm wearing my little Hawaiian-print flip-flops. If I was barefoot, my brother would save me from the melting magma of the roadway with a piggyback ride. Today, with my feet protected, I am flanked by my sister and brother, my little hands in theirs. Every time we come to a curb, they swing me by my arms, helping me over the ledge. I'm pretty sure I could make it over the curb just fine, but I like being the baby of the family, protected by the sibling security squad.

My reward for the extra paces my little legs have to make to keep up is the summer scent of pool chlorine and the sounds of cheerful screams of swimmers already in the water. We settle down poolside and unpack our bags. Mine is really just an empty backpack so I can carry it and look like my bag-toting companions. Jan stealthily pulls something from her bag, teasing me with little peeks. "Michelle! I brought you a surprise!"

She's always showering me with cool gifts, making me feel even more special and loved than my whole family already makes me feel. Jan strings out my imagination and impatient anticipation using Earl to block my view while she lures my surprise from the lair of her bag. Finally, she unleashes my surprise right there in the enchanted forest of the community pool.

It is an inflatable pool ring.

It is a dragon.

It.

Is.

Horrifying.

The entire dragon is the color of dried blood, presumably from its last meal, which could only have been another unsuspecting five-year-old.

The serpent's body is a suffocatingly restrictive ring from which even a sorcerer couldn't escape. Jutting upward is the beast's six-foot-long neck and head. His incisors are obviously the utensils with which the dragon devours his prey.

My sister caters to the dragon's hunger, casting an evil spell of imprisonment upon me, tethering me to the savage reptile and shoving me into the middle of the pool. My brother and sister point and laugh at me from their refuge of dry land.

The pool's chlorine desalinates my tears as they break the levee of my eyes. I scream deafening pleas for help that fall on, well, deaf ears. Nearby responsible adults do not notice my distress. It seems I am but a jester in their pool of mockery.

I black out for the rest of the torture session, the grateful beneficiary of memory suppression. The next thing I remember is the forced march back home, my backpack no longer empty. It is now a rucksack, laden with the very enemy that slaughtered my pool experience. The beast has also started a disintegration of my perception of the relationship between my siblings and me. We are not the equals I thought us to be. I am the target of their aggression, each attack another battle in the overall war against this new invader of their once perfect life.

That blood-red devil's wicked ambush reminds me that I am no one's "plus one" choice to the family party. This single trip to the pool is a formative immersion into the reality of my sibling hierarchy.

I submerge myself in that truth as I wade toward adulthood. I fight to untether that memory's significance from a healthy relationship with my siblings, but the undertow of that pool experience threatens to drown me.

One day, decades away from that influential summer, floating in volumes of old family photos, I discover a lifeline.

I hold a photo of a younger (and much cuter) me, clearly ready for a trip to the pool with my family. Tiny Hawaiian-print flip-flops on my feet and an oversized backpack hanging from my body's small frame, the open zipper revealing the bag's empty cavern.

The most deceitful detail of the photo is in the arms of the younger me…a detail that capsizes the current that has narrated much of my life.

My little arms lovingly clutch "Dray Dray," my light purple dragon smiling in preparation for an afternoon in the pool with his petite princess. Seeing Dray Dray breaks a self-constructed dam, unleashing a flood of positive sibling memories that don't involve sister abuse or a near drowning. I had spoiled the memory of a great summer at the pool because I dwelled on a few moments when I was frightened.

Holding the undeniable proof in my hand, it dawns on me: this isn't the first time I have misremembered an event from my past, blown it out of proportion and harbored negative emotions toward the people involved in the heinous misrepresentation.

I am grateful for the photo. It has facilitated a reunion with Dray Dray and proved me to be an inaccurate reporter. It also forces me to review my history. How often have I overinflated an incident from the past without accurate recollection to put it in perspective?

Sometimes, we just have to search for those photos and slay those dragons that threaten to drown us.

When was a time you misunderstood or misremembered an event?

Flailure

Just as important as looking back and reflecting is looking forward and preparing. Visualizing ourselves going through a routine helps prepare us as we develop new skills. Some of the people who leverage the benefits of visualization include: Olympians, musicians, astronauts, water sommeliers, performers, doctors, architects, jugglers and salespeople.

You know who else employs this tactic? Pilots.

Air Force pilot training. Del Rio. A city of 35,000 in Southwest Texas. Days are spent locked in the uncomfortably warm cockpit of a trainer aircraft built in the 1950s (which smells just as musty, dank and sock-from-gym-class as you would expect a 1950s vehicle to smell).

Nights are filled doing one of two things.

One is studying the four-inch thick technical manuals of those stinky trainer aircraft. The manuals describe how to fly the plane in such detail it might as well be a blueprint for how to build the plane.

The other thing we're doing if we're not in the air or in the books is visualizing, except we call it "chair flying." Chair flying is done while sitting in your home office or dining room or at a really long red light. I suppose chair flying could also be done while waiting to discern if a water sommelier is a real thing (it is).

That chair becomes the aircraft's ejection seat.

That footrest becomes the plane's rudder pedals.

Everything in reach is an exact replication of the cockpit switches, gauges and handles.

We chair fly checklists and aerial maneuvers.

But tonight is a rare Friday night before a Saturday when we aren't flying, so I head to the local dance club, which is a country-music bar, because…Southwest Texas.

In a male-dominated occupation like "pilot" and a male-dominated organization like "Air Force," the number of men eclipses the number of women (only 6% of all the pilots in the world, civilian and military, are women). Adding that to the facts that I don't mind country music, am eager to pull my head out of the technical manuals for a night and am willing to put my two left feet on the dance floor, I mirage into an ideal country swing dance partner for Aaron, another student pilot in my class.

Our trips to the Friday night dance floor become a regular routine. Over time, Aaron has trained me not to lead (up until the third drink, I'm gonna lead), and we have built up quite a bevy of moves. Each move has a visual signal or a single word communicating what he wants me to do (besides not lead). With just a nod or a syllable, I might be sliding between his legs, spinning on my butt in a full 360 and flipping over his arm.

I should clarify, that's not one move. I was explaining three separate positions.

Sorry, one more clarification. Not "positions." These are dance moves.

Done on a dance floor.

In public.

Fully clothed.

(I feel like I'm just making it worse.)

Tonight, Aaron meets me at the bar where I'm warming up (read: drinking).

"Mo, I have a new move for us to try!" His excitement is visible (not like that…I told you we're fully clothed) and contagious (definitely not like THAT).

"Sure! Whatever you want!" Wow, drinks must be strong tonight. Rarely do I agree to something before knowing what the something is!

Aaron begins explaining the new move, and it goes like this.

The signal is his two hands out, palms up. At which point, I jump into his arms, legs on either side of him, reach back and grab a hold of his wrists. Once wrist lock is confirmed, he lowers his arms like a forklift, I throw back my head, flip backwards and transition seamlessly onto our next move.

Simple.

We head out to the dance floor and make a couple rotations to clear the cobwebs and run through our repertoire of moves. Once Aaron has confirmed I won't try to lead, he signals for the new move.

As soon as I see the palms of his hands outstretched, I jump into his arms with my legs on either side of him. But I do not reach back.

I.

Panic.

Instead of reaching back and grabbing hold of his wrists, I place a death grip around his neck.

Just to be sure we're all seeing the same picture here:

Aaron and I are on the dance floor.

We are in an awkward embrace.

My legs are on either side of Aaron (I think the word we're looking for is "straddling").

My legs are straight out.

My legs are in Aaron's arms (which anatomically means my ass. is. in. Aaron's. palms.).

Oh, and of course, the horse collar I have around his neck.

Aaron, the ultimate professional, continues spinning us around the dance floor while my rigid legs on either side of Aaron knock dance floor neighbors out of the way.

Instead of calling for a new move, he tries to get us out of the current one, screaming, "Let go!"

I want to let go, but my mouth utters what my body is already screaming, "No!"

We start a speedy, dizzying exchange that takes us halfway around the dance floor and takes out half of the dancers on the floor.

"You have to let go!"

"I know!"

"Then let go!"

"I can't!"

Finally, we un-entwine, plucking out strands of jumbled dance partners tangled by our centrifugal force demonstration.

I'll cut to the chase and let you know that Aaron and I never attempted that move—ever again. In fact, we never spoke of it again. It's very Dance Club. And as you might already know, the first rule of Dance Club is, of course, you never talk about Dance Club.

We failed to plan for something that should have been rehearsed before it was performed (like, several times... over a very soft surface). If we had put that dance move through a quick chair flight, we might not have crashed and burned like we did.

Our failure led to flailure.

In my daily life, I often look forward to future events. Sometimes I don't do much in the way of planning and instead opt to just address things as they come, because I know I can rarely predict what will happen. I have learned, however, that I can anticipate gaps and prepare by chair flying the future event to make smarter choices and respond to different possibilities.

So when I jump into open palms with outstretched legs, I'll be ready to grab hold of the wrists, flip backwards and transition seamlessly onto my next move.

How has "chair flying" helped you successfully execute something?

Mommy, I Wanna Hold Your Hand

Opportunities to anticipate and prepare also exist on metaphorical dance floors. The rhythmic steps of life can't always be choreographed, so there are times we're out there dancing alone (and if you're dancing with yourself, well, oh, oh, oh, oh, you're my idol). But sometimes, we wanna dance with somebody, we wanna feel the heat…nope, too far.

The point I'm trying to dance to is that sometimes we need a partner to help reveal the chances around us to be a better us.

It's the end of a workday, one more day until a much-needed weekend. I'm at the mailroom on post to feed the unemployed carrier pigeons in my message box. It's lonely as an Air Force officer assigned to an Army post, but the garrison's location in Stuttgart, Germany doesn't garner much sympathy.

I'm a salmon swimming against the current of returning mailroom visitors. Smiling faces flaunt care packages, letters and cards. Among them is a woman juggling car keys in one hand and a small stack of mail in the other. Several paces behind her and taking half steps to catch up is a young girl, maybe six or seven years old. It seems safe to presume the little one belongs to the woman, since she's calling her "Mommy."

"Mommy, I wanna hold your hand," the little one whines, holding out her tiny hand to bridge the ever-increasing gap between her and Mom.

"Honey! Keep moving, we have a lot to do." Mom is very clearly on a mission.

"Pleeeeeeaaaaaaasssssseeeee?"

"Baby, come on!"

The daughter resigns herself to a familiar response, rejection slowing her little strides as she hangs her head and begrudgingly complies with the family commander.

I watch the two of them as an outsider, a childless woman never having heard the tick of a biological clock with a procreation alarm. I have several friends with children well beyond the "Mommy, I wanna hold your hand" phase. Those spawn have relocated to the demanding land of "Hey, chauffeur lady, drop me off at my destination a few blocks away, will ya?"

I weigh my mother-daughter foresight against a live-and-let-live course of inaction. Plus, I have days' worth of no mail to not collect. And I can't think of many parents who welcome the unsolicited parenting advice from a childless lesbian. But the little girl's disappointment melts my sense of what's appropriate and evaporates socially understood boundaries.

Contrary to every mother's admonition that she has eyes in the back of her head, the little girl's mom doesn't see when I do an about face, fall into formation with the little girl and grab her hand. I tell the little human, "Someday soon, your mom will be begging <u>you</u> to hold <u>her</u> hand." The little hand tightly grips mine, her sluggish pace rejuvenates into a defiant march and soon we are keeping up with Mom.

Mom looks down at her precious daughter, hand in hand with the giver of unsolicited parenting advice. She rearranges her car keys and mail to free up a hand and our short-term family of three completes the trip to their car, hand in hand.

Every day has moments providing us with opportunities to be our best. We may have to slow our pace, juggle our mail and hold someone's hand, but the good news is that it won't always be that way.

Or maybe that's the bad news.

Either way, right now is the one moment we won't get back. Let's not just mail it in.

Name a time you intervened to show
someone a new perspective.

Fight for Centerline

That mother-daughter intervention is the proudest moment of my life. It's a pivotal milestone for me, marking the moment I realized I had a perspective to provide, even if it was for a situation I hadn't exactly been through.

Just like my mom was one of the best swim coaches I ever had. And I should mention that my mom is afraid of the water and cannot swim. She was able to see and critique things about my swim stroke that didn't require her to be a swimmer. I would have missed opportunities for improvement had I discounted her inputs just because she wasn't a proficient swimmer herself.

Accepting swim tips from a woman who couldn't swim gave me an ability to absorb techniques regardless of the skills on my instructor's resume. And that aptitude floated through my life and came in handy when I landed in pilot training.

I'm in the cockpit of an Air Force trainer jet during a muggy Del Rio, Texas summer. A qualified instructor pilot sits to my right, closer than an arm's length away in an already suffocatingly confined space. We have a duplicate set of controls, but it's my hands on the stick and throttles as we come in for our third landing attempt of the day.

My eyes are focused on the 150-foot-wide patch of asphalt in front of us, less than a quarter of a mile away and getting closer. My breath quickens as I suck in all the oxygen my mask will dole out. The rubber mask, attached to my helmet, is clamped tightly over my face, trapping the olfactory blend of jet fuel, pure oxygen and the sweat of a student pilot desperately trying to earn her wings.

The control tower radio call barks a not-unfamiliar command into my helmet earpieces, "ON FINAL— GO AROUND!"

This means I'm not allowed to land, but I can come around and try landing again.

The pilot next to me grunts, "My aircraft!" jerking the stick of his dual controls to indicate he is now in charge of the plane.

He slams the throttles forward, achieving escape velocity from my poor performance and his frustration. As we accelerate safely away from the ground, he verbalizes what the control tower cannot say over the air, "Barrett! Are you even looking outside the cockpit? Can't you see you're not lined up on centerline! PULL. YOUR. HEAD. OUT!"

Air Force pilot training is when I discover I am exceptional...ly bad at landings. I hold the distinct honor of being the first person in my class of 21 pilot candidates to receive the grade of "Unsatisfactory" for a flight because of my landings. I also hold the distinct honor of being the second person in my class of 21 pilot candidates to receive the grade of "Unsatisfactory" for a flight because of my landings.

There's an adage that any landing you can walk away from is a good one. I'm just not clear if limping is considered a walk, because most of the instructors who have flown with me have a near-permanent limp as their badge of proof. Each unsatisfactory landing shortens the list of instructor pilots who are physically unbruised enough to fly with me, and each unsatisfactory grade puts me one flight closer to NOT becoming a pilot.

So, if I am going to be a pilot, I'm going to have to figure out this landing thing.

The most memorable part of my landing seems to be the *actual* landings, which make quite an impression...by making quite a *com*pression on the spine. All instructor feedback includes four-letter words and a verbal contract to never, ever fly with me again, so help them God.

Instructors attribute my airplane-bouncing finish to my poor runway alignment during final approach.

Admittedly, trying to line up on a runway a mile and a quarter long when it's five miles away seems like a lower priority than ensuring the safe control of a two-ton aircraft putting out 2,000 pounds of thrust slowing to 125 mph for landing. But, since the people telling me alignment will help with landing are wearing the silver pilot wings I covet, I decide there might be some credence to the hypothesis.

The next day, I'm sitting in an empty flight planning room. My eyes scan one wall completely consumed by a magnetic dry erase board that displays the flying schedule. Magnetic strips bear the last name of my pilot training classmates who are out slipping the surly bonds of earth because they, unlike me, have grasped how to land a plane.

The "Barrett" tag sulks alone in the "unassigned students" section at the bottom right corner of the board. An optimistic, yet-to-be-bruised instructor walks in. He grabs the magnetic representation of me and snaps it onto the board, making a magnetic commitment that he is heroically willing to step into a jet with me after the requisite preflight briefing.

We sit at a small table, a blank piece of paper between us.

I know he's writing down everything to do with landing a plane. So rather than stare at the same information every other instructor has relayed, I commiserate with my magnetic puck. I gaze at its lonely representation as the only ground-bound student pilot.

"Barrett, are you paying attention?" My current instructor interrupts my pity party.

"Yes, sir," I lie.

I decide to comply and see he is, in fact, drawing the only landing technique any instructor ever teaches: "centerline, aimpoint, airspeed." The mantra is just a reminder to pick and aim at a point at the end of the runway, controlling your airspeed until you get to the aimpoint, where you begin your transition to land.

Every instructor taught centerline, aimpoint, airspeed.

Every student understood centerline, aimpoint, airspeed.

Except me.

I drift off, wondering what job I'll have in the Air Force since the odds of being a pilot are against me. Then I hear my instructor mention something unusual.

I look down at the sketch on the paper between us. I see the runway, the centerline, an "x" for the aimpoint and…something else. He has drawn what looks like a barn on the end of the runway. Not *at* or *near* the end of the runway, *on* the end of the runway.

My surprise (and concern) is evident as I confirm, "Is that a barn?"

"Yup."

"What about 'centerline, aimpoint, airspeed'?"

He explains (for a second time, since clearly I missed the first pass at this landing technique), "The centerline is your *most important focus*. You have to land on centerline to keep the plane on the runway and clear of obstacles beyond the runway."

"And the barn?"

"That imaginary barn will help focus your efforts on the centerline. Put your aimpoint right inside those front doors. And when you get there, fly through the barn, then transition to land."

Outwardly, I nod at this novel technique.

Inwardly, my head shakes incredulously at the additional task he is demanding of me.

Landing a plane already includes a ton of things. Compensating for the wind. Listening and responding to air traffic control. Looking out for other aircrafts being flown by other unqualified pilot wannabes. Dealing with the quirks of *that* particular plane on *that* particular day. Quieting the chatter inside my head doubting me in my own fight to become a pilot.

Oh, and of course, remembering to pull my head out.

And now this guy is adding *a barn* to my cross-check?

With so few people willing to get in a plane with me, I have to be willing to try anything, no matter how ridiculous it seems. So the crazy barnstormer and I head out to the plane. He does the first takeoff and demonstrates a landing, talking us through the barn as he executes a graceful, soft landing.

And then it's my turn.

I take off. I could do that.

Now, I'm coming in to land.

Aimpoint—picked out.

Airspeed—under control.

Centerline—eh, well, close enough. This is government work after all.

My instructor reminds me of the barn (as if I could forget), and my imagination completes the details: rust-red paint peeling off the wooden sides, daylight flooding in through the far open doors, trace scents of hay and manure blend with that fragrance of jet fuel, oxygen and desperate student pilot sweat.

This barn even has a backstory complete with a farmer, her crops and her asshole neighbor slowly encroaching on her property.

But there's no time for that. This is just about the barn.

I aim for the front doors of the barn and duck as we enter (I can't be the only one who makes their vehicle lower by crouching down when entering a parking garage). I glide through the long barn, my eyes trained on the back of the barn where I picture sunlight piercing the darkness.

I get to where my instructor's barn had ended (we used the same architect), ready to start my transition to land.

But there is no transition to land, because in the midst of all that barnstorming, I have already landed. I have touched down gracefully on centerline and only once. No bounce, no bruise.

We beat up the pattern for another hour with no different results. Every time I use the barn technique, I have perfect landings. No one outside the cockpit has to order me to go around and try another landing. No one inside the cockpit has to take control and fly the plane. I am able to concentrate my focus and overcome the distractions that had prevented me from staying lined up and landing gently on centerline.

After the flight, my instructor and I stare quizzically at each other. He doesn't understand how I had earned my landing reputation, and I don't understand why no one else has taught me this technique. His ownership of my inability to land a plane and his ability to think outside the barn gave me a new perspective and approach. The mechanics of how to land a plane hadn't changed; my ability to execute those procedures had.

Everyone else only needed centerline, aimpoint and airspeed.

I needed a barn.

Because my instructor varied his approach of instruction, he changed my perspective and altered my professional trajectory. Shame on me for not realizing then how pivotal that instructor was in my career path. We may never know what small piece of advice or detail connects the dots in someone else's world.

Changing our perspective and approach doesn't apply just to landing a plane. It also applies to our life of self-discovery. We read books on leadership, listen to podcasts on self-improvement, devour articles about discovering our true self and subscribe to groups facilitating personal problem-solving.

When we vary our sources of knowledge, we improve the chance of meeting someone who provides a slightly different perspective that makes all the difference, that person who puts a barn on the end of our runway.

And if you are that someone who only needs centerline, aimpoint and airspeed, then my hope is you'll share your perspective with others. By sharing our own techniques, we develop a deeper and longer-lasting understanding of the subject or task, leveraging our cumulative knowledge and experience.

And who knows? That little piece of information you possess could be the flight plan to help someone else take off (or land).

Your fresh approach might be their barn.

So continue your flight and Fight for Centerline.

What's a technique you learned for a skill that was different than any other instructors taught you?

Plain Misunderstanding

Sharing our perspective with others and being receptive to the perspectives of others helps us cross the threshold to better understanding.

My partner, Jen, and I just bought a new home, and the final accouterment we need is a knocker for the front door. We're both pilots, so it shouldn't be a surprise that we are in the market for a door knocker in the shape of an airplane. An airplane door knocker will suitably prepare any visitor for the gallery of aviation prints, posters and memorabilia they're about to enter.

Actually, as I type this, it sounds like more of a museum than gallery.

Serendipitously, we find a store that specializes in door knockers.

I think the owner missed a huge opportunity to call the place "nice knockers," but I have the maturity of a 12-year-old, so I keep that gem to myself.

Jen and the owner have a quick dialogue that I watch from the sidelines.

Jen flies right to the point. "We're looking for a plane knocker."

"Oh, we have plenty of those." Ms. Knocker's voice reeks of dissatisfaction, as if to say her entire business model was predicated on providing a product her clientele could get nowhere else. And who are we to come crashing into her domain with a request just as easily filled by Lowe's or Home Depot (author gains no commission or compensation from the aforementioned retailers).

We, on the other hand, are thrilled because neither Lowe's, Home Depot nor Amazon had much in the way of airplane door knockers, the last piece of equipment for our aviation bunker. We follow the owner to the very back of the store, passing by racks of the best brass door knockers, you know, the breast ones. Passing by dragonflies, pineapples and sailboats, we finally arrive at a shelf of simple, dull, ordinary door knockers.

With a wave of her hand, Ms. Knockers dismissively says, "Here ya go."

Jen now takes on the tone of disappointment, our trip seeming like a total bust, "These aren't plane knockers."

"Yes they are."

"We're looking for plane knockers!"

"These ARE!"

"There is not one single plane knocker on this wall!"

"These are ALL plain knockers!"

And with the substitution of one vowel, I immediately see the sea of misunderstanding that I hear here.

I could earn a medal for my mettle as a communication clarifier: "Ma'am, my partner and I are looking for an airplane door knocker."

Ms. Knockers grounds our search for an airplane door knocker, "Oh, I'm sorry, we don't have any of those."

Jen knew exactly what she was saying and so did Ms. Nice Knockers, but neither one of them was saying the same thing. They were just talking past and over each other.

Watching this plain-plane fight, I realize the individual biases we carry with us can sometimes fly us into chambers of misunderstanding. Our histories, experiences and influencers dictate our biases. If we're not careful, those biases can get squeezed through unchecked and unverified, which can lead to plain misunderstandings.

What's the best knock-knock joke you've heard?

30 Inches

Speaking of squeezing, military members are required to have a heightened level of physical fitness, which is assessed twice a year. For the Air Force, it's a timed mile-and-a-half run and as many push-ups and sit-ups as you can do in a minute. Before all that happens, there is the favorite "let's-see-how-snug-those-pants-really-are" waist measurement. Combined with the official recording of your height and weight, the waist measurement is part of the formula to capture your body fat percentage.

There's very little that's pleasant about the biannual (not to be confused with a much more preferred "biennial") physical training test. The waist measurement, however, is my least favorite as it can be a bit subjective... depending on the bearer of the measuring device, the measurerer(er).

As with all things military, there are instructions for the taking of the waist measurement. In fact, like all things military, you have to be qualified to be a waist measurement taker. In the waist measurement taker training, you learn to completely remove the measuring tape from the body before taking each of the three separate measurements of the mid-body circumference. The average of the three measurements is entered in the body-fat gonculation.

The gonculator's body-fat percentage is crucial. Being on the wrong side of the allowable cutoff could mean needing a waiver for continued service or having to attend weight management classes or being denied a promotion or even being kindly ordered to seek employment elsewhere. All I'm saying is that most people dread the physical fitness test, but for those close to the "overweight" or "obese" body mass indices, it's a significantly dreaded event.

I use the waist measurements as a benchmark of the impact of my caloric intake. I tried (past tense) to keep below a 30-inch waist when I was in the Air Force and, as each year passed, I always felt more nervous that I was encroaching on that. On the back half of my career, relegated to more sedentary, paper-pushing jobs and the biological decrease of my metabolic rate, the waist measurement aspect of the physical fitness assessment became more and more dreaded.

Today, the small, tight-knit, mostly male unit of which I am the commander is taking the physical fitness test. Before we head out to the track to run, push-up, and sit-up, we're doing the body mass index measurements. For some mathematical wizards, the "score" they get from the body fat percentage informs just how fast they have to run the mile and a half and/or how many push-ups or sit-ups they need to do.

As a nutritional wizard, the "score" I get from the body fat percentage simply informs how much celebratory pizza I can eat later.

Another aspect regulating the waist measurement (which you learn about in waist measurement taker training) is the gender of the waist measurer. The preference is for the measurer to be of the same sex, although this could be waived with verbal consent.

And issued as part of the waist measurement taker training is your very own measuring tape. It's the kind of malleable plastic or cloth ruler you would see draped around the neck of a tailor or seamstress.

As the only female testing today, I verbally consent to have a male take my waist measurement.

No big deal.

No one can find the standard-issue, waist-measuring tape, so a resourceful, get-er-done member of the squadron comes out of the back shop with a measuring tape. It's the kind of retractable metal-bladed ruler you would see clipped on the belt of a carpenter or construction worker.

Minor deal.

I hoist up my shirt and expose my area to be measured. The male measurer wraps the cool, sharp-edged metal ruler around my midsection. Without uttering the first measurement, he snaps the button to loudly retract the stiff metal ruler to reset for the second measurement. Turns out he's an internal processor, capable of holding three measurements silently in his memory.

Measurements 2 and 3 happen similarly and I'm anxious to know if I've managed to stay at or below my 30-inch goal.

Having already waived all sorts of standard procedures, my male measurer waives one more: discretion.

Typically the measurer writes down the waist circumference on the score sheet, but today we have a separate recorder…on the other side of the room. And there's no quiet or discreet way to pass off the information with that kind of formation. So my measurer yells my waist measurement to the recorder.

And I could have lived with that, maybe. But it was the number he sent across that startled me the most.

"TWO AND A HALF FEET!" he yelled.

Holy pizza slice!!!! Two and a half feet? How badly had I let myself go? I mean, things have felt a little snug around the waist, but two and a half feet???

The taste of frustration and disappointment starts consuming my body. Ironic penance for all the calories my body has consumed. Immediately following that course is a platter of annoyance and impending reprimand. The dish of truth served by my waist measurer starves my ability to remain professional.

Keeping my mouth shut, I move aside so the next guy can get measured with the cold indiscriminate truth of the ruler. Then I calculate the difference between two and half feet and 30 inches.

The difference is…perspective. Because two and a half feet is the same as 30 inches.

While I would have preferred hearing my waist measurement taker yell "30 inches" across the room, there was nothing mathematically incorrect in his chosen articulation of how big around I was.

There are so many ways to present information in life. And there are different ways to express the same piece of information. It's better when we take the time to listen, think and check our perception before we react.

And when it comes to earning the celebratory pizza, it's best to chew and digest before we spit out and judge.

Pick a measurement, emotion or object
and write down 10 different ways to
express it.

You Gonna Eat That?

There's a shared misery about the military's annual physical fitness assessment. The strenuous nature of deployed and combat environments provide more organic opportunities for staying in tip-top shape, but most of us at some point in our careers have to serve a few sentences in the less physically demanding staff jobs.

People have different opinions about working in military staff jobs, like the ones at the Pentagon and other headquarter-type facilities. Especially for people who normally work in or around a cockpit or on the ground in foreign countries, pushing paper and attending lengthy meetings that would have been one short e-mail is met with great resistance.

I enjoy my staff jobs as well as my pilot or ground-pounding jobs. Sure, the spirit of camaraderie is more intense in an aircraft or combat zone, but there's still a sense of support and teamwork that happens in office settings. Like the office setting of my current forward operating location of the Pentagon.

Far from the tropical humid vegetation of Southeast Asia or the arid landlocked mountainous terrain of Afghanistan, we are in the dangerous concrete jungles of Rosslyn, Virginia. Whereas pilots and on-the-ground combatants have to deal with the perils of airborne engine fires or improvised explosive devices, the work setting of the urban "Pentagon overflow" environment includes crosswalks with inattentive and unyielding drivers and the high potential for paper cuts.

My predictable calendar of regular staff meetings and other standing appointments frees me up to go to the gym at 3:30 pm on the nose. This gives me enough time to get to the gym and push some weights around or shock my heart rate with something more demanding than sitting. While we don't have convenient access to the Pentagon's world-class gym, we do have a partnership with a commercial gym down the street.

The problem with a near-the-end-of-the-day workout time is that I spend most of the day coming up with all the reasons I can't go to the gym. I like working out, I know it's good for me, I know I'll feel better when I'm done and I'm fine once I get there. But getting out the office door and into the gym door is the toughest exercise of my workout.

Enter Kevin.

Kevin is another Air Force officer. He and I are both familiar with the Air Force's required physical fitness assessment and the ensuing necessity of staying on top of daily physical fitness. Kevin is my workout buddy whose mission is just to get me TO the gym. I am more motivated by punishment-based boosts, like becoming overweight or failing my physical fitness assessment, so I order Kevin to make comments about my weight at approximately 3:20 pm on my gym days.

Compliantly and punctually on Mondays, Wednesdays and Fridays, Kevin alludes to possible weight gain. As a very kind soul, Kevin obeys my request but balances it with enough levity to let me know he doesn't believe what he's saying while being convincing enough to put some doubt in my mind as to whether he *might* believe what he's saying.

Kevin is good for my humility, good for my gym loyalty and indirectly, good for my waistline. What is not good for my waistline are the cookies brought around the office this afternoon at 2:30. And they are my favorite: oatmeal raisin.

"Take two! I made plenty!" My coworker extends the plate of warm home-baked cookies.

"Don't mind if I do!" These cookies are just the treat I need for the day I've had.

Enter Kevin.

Staring at the pair of oatmeal-raisin dumbbell substitutes in my hand, Kevin judgingly asks, "Are you really gonna eat that?"

Kevin, my compliant workout buddy, is an hour early in providing the negative motivation I have requested.

"KEVIN!" Our cookie-wielding coworker yells his name in shock at the exact same time and in the exact same tone as me.

She is aghast at Kevin's inappropriate comment, and I am aghast at Kevin's premature timing.

"What?" Kevin innocently shrugs. "I'm just following orders! I thought you told me to make those comments to get you to the gym. Isn't that what you wanted?"

"IT IS!" I confirm, shards of oatmeal cookie flying out of my mouth plosively. "But I can't go to the gym for another hour and now I have to sit here and feel fat and bad about myself!"

"Oh," Kevin resigns with a sigh.

As I eat the cookies in protest of my self-imposed forcing function, I realize I have baked an artificial ingredient of accountability into Kevin's day. And with the best of intentions, he strayed from the recipe in trying to shove the lumpy batter of my body into a workout that had not been preheated. If I had enough discipline to get myself to the gym and enough willpower to turn down the cookies, I wouldn't be putting Kevin in that chewy situation.

"Seriously, are you gonna eat that?" Kevin repeats, eyeing the oatmeal cookie I have yet to lift to my mouth.

Smiling, I hand the cookie to my workout buddy.

"Thanks!" Kevin walks away, hoisting the cookie victoriously.

I may not have made it to the gym (I think I got a paper cut that needed attention), but it was a great workout anyway.

Kevin is still my gym buddy. I'll get to there tomorrow, because today, I'm eating the cookie.

Name some goals you've set that have been made better with an accountability buddy.

Flurried Display of Friendship

One place I can count on delectable food and copious drink is with my friends. And because I've been lucky enough to live next door to and around generous and hospitable neighbors, I don't need to travel far to be amongst friends. Fences may delineate physical boundaries of our properties, but the benevolence of the people living on either side of us is what delineates a merely residential area from a communal neighborhood. We are not only neighbors, we are friends. We take care of each other. We look out for each other.

Tonight, a heavy blanket hugs my sleepy body as I drift off to sleep, rekindling the memories of our evening's fire pit. We had hosted the first outdoor fire of the season and our friends from around the cul-de-sac surrounded our hardscaped fire ring.

Open bedroom windows permit an autumn breeze to glide into the room. The air carries the message of the season's change from brutal summer humidity to crisp fall temperatures. A gentle and steady rain drums pleasing rhythms on the surfaces of our roof, road and driveway.

The scent of wet pavement fuses with the fragrance of recently extinguished fires. The fires are another indicator of the transition into fall, blazing beacons drawing residents from the cooled comfort of air-conditioned interiors for the warmth of an outdoor flame.

The sound of distant sirens begin to compete with the rain for aural attention. A prominent hospital located two miles away not surprisingly attracts emergency response vehicles. The wails of these sirens *increase* in volume, meaning the distance between us is *decreasing*, ferrying curiosity about their destination.

Doubt mobilizes.

Had our fire really been extinguished?

We assumed the incoming rains that broke up the neighborhood party would quench the flames we had only recently gathered around. Was it possible the same autumn breeze lulling me to sleep caused sparks to dance out of the bounds of the fire ring?

The screams of the sirens arrest any cardiac calm I have. Curiosity is the primary patient now. I jump out of bed and check the backyard fire pit. Flames tango with the rain, a choreographed tease of the fire's spirit, daring the rain to smother her.

I shuffle to the front window.

My eyes confirm a nagging suspicion.

I see smoke rising from our neighbor's roofline.

Oh, crap.

"GET UP! GET UP! GET UP!" The blaring Klaxon of my voice alerts Jen that it's go time.

She doesn't question our mission, but I clarify anyway, "Neighbor's house is on fire!"

We know we can beat the fire trucks to our neighbor's home. Our unprofessional life-saving skills administered now are better than well-trained first responders' efforts later. This is the time to act.

I am the first one down the carpeted steps leading to our front door, with Jen in tight formation behind me.

I throw open the front door and my response is literally obstructed by the reminder that we had locked the exterior glass door.

I careen right into it.

And when I say Jen is in tight formation behind me, I mean tight.

She slams into me, pressing my face into a distorted caricature against the glass.

Frantic, incoherent instructions and a brief, unproductive round of blame game ensue.

We masterfully decipher the front door lock. We sprint out, hurdle our shrubs and charge the short distance to our neighbor's front yard.

As the lead responder, I slam on my brakes.

As the confused wingman, still in tight formation, Jen slams into me.

Despite no glass door to sandwich me, this collision reeks of a *Keystone-Cops*-meets-*The-Three-Stooges* spectacle. My mind gathers the pertinent information, dismissing the parody of our response.

Did I smell smoke?

Yes.

Did I hear sirens?

Yes.

Were the sirens getting louder?

Uhm, not anymore.

Did I see fire?

Well, yea, but in the fire ring.

Did I see fire on the neighbor's roof?

No.

But I did see smoke.

Or something that looked like smoke.

Like steam.

Like steam that would rise from a roof that had been heated by the sun and then cooled by something like…rain.

Well, crap again.

Jen dutifully follows me as I sulk the long way home through our neighbor's driveway, to the sidewalk, to our driveway, skipping the shrub jump and glass door–smash steeplechase. The lengthy 30-second walk gives me reassurance that we have done the right thing, erring on the side of action and compassion.

I sleep soundly, covered by the blanket of neighborly friendship and caring, resting on a duvet of comic relief provided by our flurried display of that friendship and caring.

Sometimes the response to the fires in our lives are just to fan the flames of friendship.

When have you overreacted to a situation out of compassion?

The First Word of That New Prescription

There is scientific evidence that overreaction is a protective evolutionary tool. So, fire or no fire, I will always be proud of my overreaction to the smell of smoke. If it *had* been a fire and Jen and I had saved a family from a burning house, we'd be heroines.

There was another time I *may* have veered *slightly* into that lane. It was the time I unsuccessfully successfully pulled rank. Yes, you read that right.

I'm stationed at the Pentagon where the words on my computer screen just weren't as sharp as they were when I had a 3 in front of my age instead of a 4. I even try different computers, but the common denominator in all my failed unofficial vision tests is me.

I knew it was time to make an appointment for an official vision test. The advantage of working in the Pentagon is we have a full complement of every service you need during the long work day. There's a bank, gift shop, barbershop, beauty shop, pharmacy, food court, dentist, jeweler, chocolate shop, florist and—pivotal to this story—an optometrist.

So I'm on my way to the Pentagon clinic to get my eyes checked by an Air Force optometrist.

The military rank structure at the Pentagon is top heavy when compared to any other military facility. There are a lot more generals and admirals walking the halls than initial-entry ranked folks. Pentagon occupants tend to be closer to AARP membership qualifying age than they do minimum legal-drinking age.

I remember the shock during my first day working in the Pentagon as a major, which is a mid-tier rank, high enough to have responsibility but low enough to evade high expectations. I stood in line at the donut shop to grab a box of breakfast for the office and happened to glance back and see a three-star admiral two people behind me. I freaked out.

In the normal military world at an average base, a colonel ruled the roost and the world stopped when the colonel, especially if it was the colonel who was the base commander, walked in. And now, there was a guy three ranks higher than that mortal and he was behind me in line to get donuts and HE WAS CARRYING HIS OWN DRY CLEANING!

What a bizarre world this was.

Having never been in such a situation before, I had no idea what the military protocol was. Should I give him my spot in line? Was I supposed to spring for his donuts? Should I offer to carry his dry cleaning?

Turns out, none of the above. Apparently, people assigned to the Pentagon are just used to the top-heavy rank structure there, understanding that generals and admirals are a dime a dozen.

Today's optometrist is a textbook example of this imbalance. As I am now years away from that first day in the Pentagon and now a colonel (who are also a dime a dozen in the Pentagon), I am unfazed by having my eyes checked by an eye doctor who couldn't even celebrate his medical school graduation with an alcoholic beverage.

Doogie Howser held the distinction of being the youngest licensed doctor in the country until my eye doctor came onto the scene. Note: if you don't know who Doogie Howser is, then you were probably kindergarten classmates with my eye doctor. So we'll just call my eye doctor Young Sheldon.

Because I am old enough to know who Doogie Howser is, and because this is my third sentence in the Pentagon, I'm used to the disproportionate rank structure and unshaken by the sight of a rube officer. And I'm hardened by the reality that I'm on the back side of my career and have officially become the "they" I used to complain about. I've also become impatient with the slow bureaucracy that I, as "they," perpetuate.

I really just need Young Sheldon to update the prescription for my reading glasses to sharpen the letters on the computer.

He dims the light, then challenges my ability to retain the mnemonic for the letters I saw with two eyes before he made me read the line with only one eye. He rolls his chair in front of me, with only a terminator endoskeleton mask and breath mint job security between us.

Then we go through what is the most stressful part for me, "Which is better, one or two? Three or four? Boxers or briefs?"

I swear it's just a test, and I'm pretty sure he's just toggling between two identical settings to give him ammo for the next optometry convention where attendees joke about how many patients fell for the "Which Is Better?" game.

After a few more rounds of "One or two? Three or four?" then a double retinal burn with a magnifying glass, the boy doctor turns up the lights.

"Everything look ok, Captain?" Calling him by his rank seems more believable than calling him "Doctor."

"Yes, ma'am."

"Sooooo, no glaucoma in there clouding up my computer screen vision?" I joke, fishing for a medical marijuana card I don't really want (it's like taking hotel mini shampoos and mouthwashes that I never use).

He grabs his prescription Post-it notes to not prescribe cannabinoids to reduce my absent intraocular pressure.

"No, ma'am, your eyes just need some assistance for both near and far vision. This is just a natural part of the aging process, ma'am."

Although he'd been professionally respectful up until now and compliant with the military rank nomenclature protocol, the subtext of his last "ma'am" had a very gentrified tone that sounded like "grandma."

I can sense he's not only gathering material for banter at the eye doctor rally (those guys really make a spectacle of themselves), but he's also playing his young man card, which makes me want to pull the tennis balls off my walker and knock the pen out of his hand before he makes the first mark on his prescription pad. I have too many friends whose eyeglasses have that telltale line in the middle of the lens that scream, "Hey! I'm so old, I'm now familiar with the word 'presbyopia!'"

I make a note to get younger friends and then get back in the higher ranking seat. "Captain, if the first word of that new prescription begins with a 'bi,' we're gonna have a problem."

The young whippersnapper quickly realizes that we're heading down a path of a story he won't want to share with his eye mentors. He's been beat, and even though he knows that I might need bifocals, such a prescription will not bode well for his military career.

"Oh no, ma'am," he stammers, ripping off the script for my reading glasses, then starting on a separate script for my distance vision glasses.

"Here ya go, Colonel." He hands me two pieces of paper for old-school bifocals, also known as two pairs of glasses.

I arrogantly take my victory prescriptions, having shamelessly pulled rank. I depart the clinic with my head held high. Or at least my head was held high until my prescription, correction, prescriptions were filled. I feebly depart the clinic with <u>two</u> pairs of glasses, realizing that, in trying to pull rank, I had been outranked by a lower-ranking officer.

Every time I have to switch glasses for near or far vision clarity, I, the Colonel, curse the Captain. Actually, I curse myself. The two pairs of glasses helped me see the problem with trying to outrank a professional.

Before my eye puns get cornea and cornea, I'll let you know that I went back and got my prescription (singular) for bifocals.

Now my dual spectacle-carrying case is half full (or is it half empty?), but I'm seeing 20/20 and will be for a long time because I plan to dilate.

What's a time you would have been
better off going with a professional's
recommendation?

Method of Birth Control

With my bifocals proudly on my face, I navigate to the Pentagon clinic for my annual physical. Like our physical fitness assessment, there are a sundry of medical procedures we can't evade in the military.

One is the annual physical. Once a year, we're hounded to come in and get poked, probed and prodded so the docs can record an official clean bill of health for anyone tracking our physical aptitude.

I've been through enough of these annual analyses that I can fill out the pre-visit paperwork with my eyes closed. Rather than do that, I try to have fun with the questionnaire. The fun is purely for my own entertainment though, because I'm pretty sure of two things: no one answers them honestly and no one actually reads them.

I offer some of my responses as proof of both.

I do answer honestly when it comes to the sliding scale answer to "I wear a seat belt every time I am in a motor vehicle" (answer: "always" only because "when my hands aren't full" isn't an available response).

I *may* adjust the scale of my answer to the question of "Per week, I have ___ many drinks." Weights and measures have never been my forte.

But my favorite question on the dating-app questionnaire, oops, pre-appointment screening survey, is "method of birth control." Such a brazen request… that I'm more than happy to satisfy.

My responses over the years of responding have included:

"Abstinence."

"Babysitting."

"Coaching youth sports."

"Good lighting."

And after it was legal, "homosexuality."

I do think, however, I would have been safe even when it was illegal because, as proof of my point, no one ever noticed, questioned or even laughed at any of my responses.

Sometimes the only person we need to make laugh is ourselves.

What's an inside joke that makes you laugh?

Postnasal Drip

Another medical procedure we can't dodge in the military is the annual flu shot.

Shots I can deal with.

The flu mist, I cannot.

I won't tell you that the live attenuated vaccine is shot up your nose with an intranasal blast of about 1,000 psi (a nail gun only needs 130 psi).

I'll skip the disgusting details of how the goo, having been shotgunned into your cranium with inexcusably excessive force, then seeps down the back of your throat, forward enough to taste the bitter, fowl fermentation of egg-based technology and too far back to do anything about it.

I won't elaborate on how your body's own mucus-making kitchen works overtime to try and ward off the hideousness of the strain of virus once incubated in chicken eggs and baby chicken kidney cells.

I will also leave out the part where the back of your eyes spasm with an itch you can't scratch while the public-facing side of your eyes water and your nose runs as basically all your facial orifices reject the repulsive concoction that could have and should have been a tasteless, speedy injection.

All I will say is that I much prefer the shot to the spray.

There are some legitimate ways of getting the shot versus the mist, including: being outside the age range of 2 to 50, having a weakened immune system, caring for an immunocompromised person, being pregnant or not having a functioning spleen. Except for the spleen thing, none of the exclusions applied to me. I mean, I have a spleen, I'm just not sure what it does and therefore whether it functions.

So, at my annual physical, I am mist-bound, unless my spleen decides to stop functioning.

The technician who kicks off the annual physical process doesn't check my spleen. She tests my eyes, checking my near and far vision, depth perception and whether I'm a candidate for medical marijuana—you know, for my glaucoma.

She shuts me in a tiny padded soundproof phone booth with only a headset, a wired Jeopardy buzzer and the instructions to buzz in every time I hear a series of three beeps. Correction. What is, "Buzz in every time I hear a series of three beeps."

A few more procedural steps to go before I'm escorted to the doctor's exam room. Today, that procedural step is the flu prophylaxis.

"Ok, ma'am." The technician hands me a tissue, a sure indication that the spray plunger is bound for my nose holes.

"Oh." I feign total surprise that the mist has even made it to the U.S. military. "Don't you have the shot?"

I figure most people are syringe-shy, so I'm happy to take one for the team and keep an intranasal applicator for the backroom supply.

"No, ma'am. Our shots don't come in until next week."

YES! This is the information I need for my shot-not-mist strategy.

I pride myself on being a pretty convincing negotiator, and as I'm about to be held hostage by an accumulation of vile live flu virus seeping down my throat, the stakes can't be much higher.

"I see. Well, I'm happy to come back next week for the shot."

"No, ma'am, we have the mist now."

As Captain of Team Shot, I employ a battle of attrition against Team Mist, figuring I can waste enough time in the verbal sparring before the tech has to lay down her spray and either stab me with the needle or bypass the vaccine altogether in order to keep the doctor on schedule.

I also employ the pulling rank tactic. I'm not proud of it, but if I have to choose between pulling rank and enduring two rounds of putrid post-nasal drip, I'll pull rank. I assure the tech I'll cover for the delay in my flu prevention and that I'll take ownership as the higher-ranking member.

The tissue the tech touted transforms to her flag of surrender, and we agree on a future date for my flu shot.

My posture is tall as I follow my recently defeated rival on a short parade to the exam room. One of the spectators along our route is Darlene, an Air Force doctor and long-time friend. It isn't until I see her in the hall that I realize our assignments have overlapped us at the same base. We do as quick of a catch-up as we can in the fleeting moments before I get escorted into another doctor's exam room (although having Darlene as my doctor would have been fun).

With a wave and an "I'll call you," I bid farewell to Darlene and take a seat in my doctor's exam room. I lean back in the chair, clasping my hands behind my head in the catapult pose, essentially body language that shouts, "One day you'll be as conniving and as in control as me." Having staked my territorial claim of the space, the technician closes the door to the room, leaving me alone to bask in the banner day I'm having. I mean, I'm not walking out with a prescription for glaucoma pot, but I'm also not sipping dreadful pharmaceutical cocktails served from my snout through the back of my throat. And I've caught up with a good friend.

And it's that good friend who barges in through the door of her colleague's exam room. No knock. No "are you decent?" announcement. The door flies open, and a whirlwind of Darlene takes over the space in my victory vortex. The tempest flies toward my eminent domain before I can unclasp my hands from behind my head. My interwoven fingers, no longer a sign of dominance, are now restraints preventing me from shielding myself from hurricane Darlene.

The storm is headed toward me, and at the eye of the storm is the violently destructive container of flu mist. Not only can I smell the barometric change in the air, I can preemptively taste the foreboding drip of the nasal spray precipitation.

Darlene violates my privacy and security even further as she plants her non-flu-mist-wielding hand firmly on the center of my chest, pushing me back into catapult position, translating the pose from dominance to submission.

I counter with a foot to her belly, but the invasive length of the flu mist applicator gives her a reach advantage. Before I know it, half a dose of the live attenuated flu virus has been injected into my left nostril.

"Other side," Darlene says in a sterile, unfeeling chair side manner.

With no time to react, my foot still in her gut and her hand still pinning me against the wall, the right flank of my nasal area is assaulted with the spray.

"Tissues are on the desk...I'll call ya later!"

And with that, just as soon as the tornado had made landfall, it was gone. There was no calm after the storm, only the post-nasal drip of a victory celebrated too early.

Name something you were forced to do that was for your own good.

Baseball

On the heels of celebrating too quickly, it seems like a perfect time for a revenge inoculation with another dose of Darlene.

Before Darlene's violating injection of "friendship," we were roommates. I had moved from Howard Air Force Base in Panama to Travis Air Force Base in Northern California. I lucked out moving in with Darlene, a college rugby teammate turned doctor on base.

It's been the typical day of in-processing briefings and running around. I come home to see a note from Darlene: "Pamela has an extra ticket for this Friday's baseball game."

I definitely want that extra ticket. After the seemingly senseless running around the base, I need that extra ticket. Pamela is a friend from Panama who moved to Travis Air Force Base a year ahead of me, so it'll be nice to reconnect with someone who's local now.

Plus, it's the middle of September and I don't want to turn down a chance to see the San Francisco Giants. And it's a game against the Padres—who doesn't love a little intrastate competition? (Intrastate? Interstate? Eh, same difference.) Irregardless and for all intents and purposes, I wanna go to the game. My mitt is with my household goods somewhere on the other side of the Panama Canal, but I figure that just frees up a hand so I can hold a beer and a hot dog.

I call Pamela. "Pamela! I got your message about Friday and I would love to go!"

She's excited, and we go through the logistics and timing. Friday can't come soon enough. I can already feel the plastic cup of cold beer sweating in my non-hot-dog-holding hand.

Then Pamela throws this curveball, "And don't forget, you have to wear mess dress."

What. The. I nearly drop my imaginary beer and hot dog…

The mess dress uniform is the Air Force's most formal, black-tie-equivalent uniform. I'm talking long, slitted skirt, tuxedo shirt, cufflinks, pantyhose and a cummerbund. None of which scream, or even remotely whisper, "baseball."

"I'm sorry, why am I wearing mess dress to a baseball game?!"

Pamela's about as confused by me talking about baseball as I am by her suggesting I wear a tux to the game. "We're not going to a baseball game, we're going to the base ball…for the Air Force birthday."

Every September, the Air Force celebrates its great 1947 divorce from the Army when the Army Air Corps split into the Air Force and the Army. And that celebration requires everyone getting dressed up, hoisting glasses of wine in endless toasts and, of course, birthday cake. You'll notice my description of the base ball has the distinct absence of beer, hot dogs and baseball.

"Uh, yeah, I'm not going to the base ball."

Thank God my mitt and mess dress were still on the other side of the Panama Canal.

And thank God the message Darlene misunderstood wasn't life or death. She is a good doctor and a good friend, just not the best relay-er of messages. Because baseball is a familiar event to her and a ball on base is not a familiar event, in that split second, she jotted down what made sense to her without feeling any need for clarification.

To be an effective communicator, we don't have the luxury of casually handing off partly accurate messages. Seek clarity as your communication currency. And if you have any questions, I'll be at the baseball field, NOT in my mess dress uniform at the base ball.

What challenges have you faced as an effective communicator?

Currency of Trust

I should be fair and cut Darlene some slack; maybe I was the one who misinterpreted her note about the baseball game/event. She is a doctor after all, and we all know about their handwriting legibility.

And speaking of fair, "The Big E" is New England's annual 17-day multistate fair, featuring barnyard animals, future farmers, purveyors of fare foods and artisans. Yankee Candle's yet-to-be-waxed "Big E" scent would be the fragrance of sweaty livestock, spun sugar, deep-fried cholesterol on a stick and freshly roasted turkey legs.

Amidst the soundtrack of screams emanating from amusement park rides that spin, twist and flip its occupants, I wander the fairgrounds while consuming the same amount of calories in one afternoon that midsized countries intake annually. Out of respect for the pigs, cattle and chickens who think they're there on a field trip, I finish my bacon-wrapped ground-beef chicken nuggets before visiting their compounds.

In a gastric stupor, I end up in one of the many vendor shops, the offline Etsy before the online Etsy was even a thing. Crafts, crap and collectables await to lighten my financial load. I find myself buying a wrought iron wall decoration, paying with a crisp $50 bill once earmarked for oversized corn on the cob, grilled in the husk, doused in butter, showered with salt and served without utensils, a napkin or dental floss.

I rush out of the vendor's small tent, anxious to get the piece of art I neither need nor want into the car so I can hurry back to stand in line with people I don't know to get on a roller coaster I don't want to ride.

"Hey!"

It could have been one of the 1.5 million people there hollering to get the attention of one of the other 1.49 million people there. Yet, somehow, I know that "hey" is for me.

And it is.

The artisan confronts me, "You paid with a counterfeit bill!"

The hell I did! I know I haven't used any counterfeit money. Knowingly…

The affront on my integrity is replaced with pissed-offness directed at the unknown forger who has duped me with fake money. The small business owner becomes the grand marshal of the parade back to her shop, the effigy of my once perfect integrity floating on display.

Back in her American-dream tent of opportunity, she pulls out my $50 bill and points at the three black lines from the counterfeit detector pen.

She grabs the pen and tries another spot on the bill.

And another.

And another.

Six strikes against me, and we're losing space on the scoreboard.

"Stop. Please. I have more money." I fan out a few $20 bills for her to choose from to cover the cost of the wrought iron decoration in which I have officially lost interest.

Having established myself as the circulator of counterfeit currency, she tests the authenticity of my $20 bill.

It is also counterfeit.

As is the next $20 bill.

And the next.

The scent of noxious marker permeates the injustice and brings clarity.

Avoiding too much condescension, I innocently ask, "When did Sharpie start making counterfeit pens?"

The short session of permanent marker huffing slows her response, but she eventually looks up like a drug addict caught in a rebound high. The rosy blush on her face is her tell of embarrassment as she pushes my $20s back at me in an "all in" manner. She releases me from her pen with a sheepish laugh, a flock of apologies, my wrought iron decor, my restored integrity and a great story.

Our intentions, regardless how pure, can get marked up by misperception, usually the result of accidental miscommunication. When we face those assaults on our reputation, we should do it with humility and grace.

Because, to be fair, we've all inadvertently circulated wrongdoing. There's just more value when we invest in a currency of trust.

**How did you react when your reputation
or integrity was challenged?**

One-Quarter Step-Japanese

People are watching how we conduct ourselves when we're misrepresented. And I'm assuming you're familiar with the joke about what happens when you assume…you're usually wrong.

We make assumptions all day long, and unless you're in the science world, you probably aren't taking the time to create, test and verify a hypothesis. Yet many of the assumptions we make on a daily basis aren't accurate. Some statistics say that 50% of the assumptions we make are wrong, but I'm only assuming that to be the truth.

Having been raised in a mixed family, I've not always noticed race and skin color. So it's hard for me to predict issues that might be due to conclusions others might jump to. My mom is 100% Asian. My dad is 100% Wisconsin-bred. My five siblings and I have the same dad, but only I have the Asian mom. As a result, I have two nieces who hilariously identify themselves as "one-quarter step-Japanese."

I'm traveling via air with my mom and niece Jess, and my niece is the only one of us three who doesn't have TSA pre-check status. As we approach the first guardian of the coveted pre-check process, Jess helps her dainty Asian grandma untangle her purse from her walker. Though no words are spoken, it's clear that Jess and Mom are familiar with each other. What is unclear is that they could be related.

The TSA agent assumes that Jess is this elderly lady's assistant and ushers Jess through to the forbidden fruit of the TSA pre-check lane, saving her from the shoe-removing, laptop-extracting, general-disrobing sequence of regular TSA screening.

As he gently hands them off to the conveyor belt team, he mouths and points that Jess is the older woman's interpreter. I suppose there have been more egregious assumptions made in the history of man. Mom has been known to play up the "little old lady with a walker" bit (how do you think she got TSA pre-check status to begin with?) but be not fooled—the woman catches more than she lets on to.

So Jess continues through the TSA pre-check line, Mom stays silent, and I watch from the recombobulation area, having already cleared security. Now I will say that Mom is deaf in one ear and, not being a frequent flier, isn't overly familiar with the ever-changing processes at the airport, so some of the confusion is legit. Jess caringly helps Mom through security, speaking slowly and closely into Mom's only hearing ear.

For whatever reason, when Mom gets to the scanner, they want her to remove her shoes (so much for expeditious security-ing). They make some nonverbal signals to try and communicate that request to my mom. I'm not sure what the gesture for "take off shoes" would be, but I know I never want this guy on my team in a game of charades. Mom looks helplessly at Jess and shrugs her shoulders as she tries to decipher whether the third base coach is miming to slide into home or get a pedicure.

Jess leans toward the man to clarify what he is trying to communicate. Quietly, he nods toward Mom and tells Jess, "Could you tell her to take off her shoes."

Jess turns to Mom and yells (in her good ear), "GRAMA, TAKE OFF YOUR SHOES!"

As Mom dutifully takes off her shoes, the TSA agent dons an "I could have done THAT" look, and said, "I thought you were her interpreter."

Jess replies over her shoulder as she expedites through security, "Nope, just her granddaughter."

This was an innocuous assumption that only led to family laughs (and this story). But so many of the wrong assumptions we make in life can lead to conflicts that can be avoided if we would just take the time to ask and seek to understand.

But if anyone ever needs an interpreter, my one-quarter step-Japanese nieces are always available.

What's a time a misunderstanding had a positive outcome?

Nice Landing Today

My niece clarifying the truth about her English-speaking grandma *after* we cleared airport security was an innocuous silence. But there are times where it really is more important to speak up and accept responsibility (before you clear the security checkpoint).

I'm on short final into Andersen Air Base on the small Pacific island of Guam, a common node from our hub in Northern California. Because we fly there frequently, I throw around the name of the U.S. territory quite, well, frequently. So much so that it catches me off guard when people aren't as familiar with the location.

For example, my soccer buddy Mike thinks I'm resorting to making up names of places to get out of hanging with him. All my "excuses" have been legitimate truths. One time, I was sent out on a three-week mission that ended up being five weeks. Another time, I was called into the squadron to cover the duties of our flight scheduler. And now, a short-notice mission to the made-up land of "Guam" ruins Mike's final proposal.

The mission involves flying cargo on the Air Force's largest strategic airlifter. The C-5 Galaxy was Lockheed's response to the military's 1964 "Heavy Logistics System" request and was often called on to transport outsized cargo around the world. Despite being a military aircraft, our missions aren't always combat-related. The C-5's behemoth carrying capacities enable it to serve humanitarian purposes as well.

On board today is the Federal Emergency Management Agency's initial disaster response team. The majority of the team is seated in the aft passenger compartment some 240-plus feet behind the cockpit. Our 143-foot cargo compartment, which boasts the quirky distinction of being one foot longer than the Wright brothers' first powered flight, is now filled with blankets, bottled water, generators and floodlights.

Guam has just been hit by super Typhoon Paka, bringing early Christmas gifts of 21 inches of rain, 35-foot waves, an island-wide power outage and $500 million of damage. A few members of the FEMA team ride up in the cockpit to get an airborne assessment as we come in to land. Sturdy palm trees bow down ahead of us, not out of subservient deference to the mighty C-5 but in defeated resignation to Typhoon Paka and her 145 mph sustained winds. The flight engineer depressurizes the cabin to gain equilibrium with the ambient air, and the humid scent of island air fills the cockpit. Normal floral bouquets welcoming us to Guam are replaced by outside air reeking of desperation with notes of anticipation for the life-saving supplies on board.

Andersen Air Base's runway is roughly 11,000 feet of asphalt and concrete. Because the runway was constructed over rough and uneven terrain, no matter which direction you land from, the downslope of the 200-foot wide runway gives the illusion of a bowl-like landing environment. To the uninitiated pilot, the illusion causes long landings. Not an ideal situation with an entire ocean at either end. Landing on the Guam air patch requires trust in your instruments and subtle power management. Even well-rehearsed pilots have the days when landings on Andersen Air Base catch them off guard, resulting in more-than-firm landings or floated landings bringing the ocean "safety net" way too close.

For two reasons, I am only running checklists and not performing the landing today. The first reason is because this is my first trip into Guam and my aircraft commander is playing the role of instructor pilot, showing his Guam-landing prowess where we neither float anxiety-inducingly near the ocean or hit the ground with tooth-rattling firmness. The second reason is because I'm in a time-out of sorts from the landing I performed at Hickam Air Force Base in Hawaii yesterday.

Landings are tricky, especially for strategic airlift aircraft. We can spend literally half days airborne before it's time to put the bird to bed. The California to Hawaii leg is about six hours, the first half of which is spent eagerly awaiting the point of no return, after which you're committed to the Hawaiian Islands. The second half is anticipation-ridden, knowing that if any malfunctions happen now, you're carrying them to Hawaii. Part of that anticipation is obvious excitement that we're Hawaii bound for a quick overnight stay that will include cooking our own steaks at the Shore Bird Restaurant. I blame the anticipatory scent of grilled beef for my poor performance on my touchdown.

Despite having the six hours to prepare myself for the landing, I essentially gave up on the final touches before touchdown. To this day, there may still be the impression of 28 tires on the runway where I planted the C-5.

In the flying world, the landing is probably the most noticeable event if it's poorly done. Anyone who's ridden on a commercial airliner knows a bad landing when they've lived through one. I have learned as a pilot to grant myself grace when I make a particularly bad landing, mostly because absolutely no one else will be doling out anything remotely representative of "grace." My Hickam, Hawaii landing is a great illustration of a very bad landing and the lack of grace from the crew.

My Hickam, Hawaii landing is firm, painful and very noticeable.

"Copilot. Jump." The third pilot sitting at the additional crew member position follows the in-aircraft interphone protocol of announcing the called crew position first, followed by the calling crew position.

"Go ahead. Jump," I call back.

"How many landings you wanna log?" Example one of the graceless support of the crew. The third pilot manages the flight's log and, while there is only a spot to log one takeoff per landing, his sarcastic point is valid.

"Copilot. Troop." This is the loadmaster in the aft passenger compartment some 240-plus feet behind where I'm sitting.

"Go ahead, Troop." I know the shit is gonna start.

"Ma'am, permission to clear off headset to reset oxygen masks?" His implication that my landing jarred all the oxygen masks out of their ceiling berths is code for "the shit hath started."

"Copilot. Flight Engineer." More shit.

"Go Engineer."

"Yes, ma'am, permission to run the unkneeling checklist?"

Asshole.

More graceless ribbing as the flight engineer implies that my definitive landing has collapsed the aircraft's unique kneeling system that allows the aircraft to lower itself to minimize the angle of the ramp for cargo onloads with close clearances.

So, every crew position has weighed in.

"Reach 9544, Tower." Time for the interplane banter to cease. This was a call from outside the plane.

"Tower, Reach 9544, go ahead." My aircraft commander, as the non-flying pilot, returns the call to the tower.

"Yea, Reach, you all ok?" followed by a brief bout of laughter, their rhetorical inquiry letting us know that they, too, witnessed the hard landing and wanted in on the lack of tenderness for my feelings.

My feelings have become accustomed to living below a protective layer of epidermis. This layer is part of the aircrew DNA, out of necessity. Maneuvering a 380,000-pound vehicle from sea level to 41,000 feet presents myriad learning opportunities. With lives on board, lives at stake and a significant financial investment with the cargo we carry, lessons come first, feelings come second.

And keeping that larger purpose in mind is essential when your latest attempt at being proficient at landing a nearly 200-ton aircraft is rewarded with compliments like, "What the f*** was that!? You pulled power too early, that's why you sank and dropped in the landing!" In the evolution of making us all better, the honesty policy was in full use and colorfully adapted over time.

Flight debriefs happen as the last step of each flight. The debrief is when any flaws that are obstacles to reaching your full potential are addressed. A debrief isn't intended to rip away a crew member's feeling of self-worth, but in trying to improve future performance, brutal honesty is required. If the flight is the last of the day, an unofficial debrief often happens over an adult beverage, which often leads to more colorful debriefs. Though they're not personal, to an outside observer, they may sound very much so. There is little room for personal feelings when the severity of your mission and the lives are in your hands.

There's a lot of pressure to prove yourself, to fit in and to get along, and that all comes with the added bonus of actually being a proficient pilot. The aircrew world has a lot of subculture rules that aren't explicitly listed anywhere, and unless you have an indoctrinated pilot taking you under their wing, you're kind of flying solo to navigate the world. So aside from being a good pilot, you also have to work at being a good crew member. The challenge is that, while piloting skills start and end in the cockpit, aircrew skills are on display all the time.

Like right now, after my aircraft commander's landing at Guam. I'm standing on the tarmac next to the FEMA mission commander as light carts, generators and pallets of bottled water are off-loaded from our plane. As the belly of the mighty C-5 empties, meaning my day is about over and the FEMA team's day is about to begin, the mission commander starts his farewells.

"Well, thanks for the ride."

"Our pleasure."

"Oh, and nice landing today." A little too much emphasis on "today," but I'm probably just reading in to that. Even though my aircraft commander wasn't nearby, I know enough about good-pilot–good-crew-member balance that I shouldn't try to steal a compliment meant for someone else (especially another pilot).

So I confess, "Well, I can't take credit for the landing, that was all the work of the other pilot."

Knowing that the "other pilot" was well outside of earshot, the FEMA mission commander nudges me like the other participant in an inside joke, "Oh. Is he trying to redeem himself from that landing in Hawaii yesterday?"

See? Anyone knows a bad landing when they've lived through one. In that split second, I saw my chance to say aloha to the stigma of the Hawaiian landing and lei the blame on my aircraft commander. But intensifying that cyclone of elements was the whole good pilot–crew-member balance. In the spirit of not wanting "dick move" included in my unofficial debrief, I confessed, "Nope. That one was mine."

The FEMA mission commander was speechless, but mostly because he had already said enough. He had verbally documented just how bad my landing had been. Not only had my landings received criticism from the crew inside the plane and the control tower outside the plane, my landing of infamy lived on in the honest judgment of a passenger a day later.

We have to accept the highs and lows of life, give credit where it's due and take blame when it's ours.

When was a time you took an "out" for accepting blame for something?

If Those Guys Can Make Moonshine

I think part of the reason I love flying a strategic airlift aircraft is because of the crew concept. Even single-seat aircraft take more than just the pilot to get it airborne. The maintainers, the crew chief, the weather forecasters, the box lunch preparers…everyone has a hand in launching that plane. And every member of that collective crew has a unique contribution.

This crew concept is something that my partner Jen and I talk about a lot. Usually over wine. We are avid wine drinkers. This is not to be confused with being wine snobs, connoisseurs or sommeliers. I just mean we drink a lot of wine. And because we deem ourselves as highly efficient people, we figure it's time to take out the middleman and start making our own wine.

We watch those TV shows about moonshiners and, not to judge a book by its coveralls, but if *those guys* can make moonshine (and have their own TV show), then certainly two checklist-oriented Air Force pilots can ferment some grapes.

We do our research, we buy a high-quality kit, we follow the checklist diligently and we bottle our first batch of wine. We wait the checklist-dictated amount of time for proper fermentation, then invite our closest friends over for a release party for our inaugural batch. This is a catered affair, and everyone is dressed up. The energy is electric, but the lighting is by candle (ironic, right?).

We satisfyingly uncork a few bottles and pour a healthy taste into everyone's glass. We make a somber toast to our future as winemakers and everyone simultaneously takes a hearty swig of our product. Also simultaneous and unanimous is the decision that this is absolutely the. worst. wine. anyone has ever tasted.

Not to be deterred, Jen and I set out on batch two. Because, still, we feel like being checklist-oriented pilots is proof that we can mash a bearded, corncob–pipe-smoking, bib-overall–wearing, illicit-moonshine–making dude (puns intended).

We do further research, buy a higher-quality kit, follow that checklist even more diligently and bottle our second batch of wine. We give this batch a little more time to ferment for good measure. For the uncorking, we invite just a couple friends and serve no food. Candles are out but not lit. We pour just a splash into each glass, make a half-assed toast and everyone takes a cautious approach to sampling batch two.

Once again, the opinions are simultaneous and unanimous. And <u>this</u> time, the verdict is that this batch…is worse than the first.

Now, I'm not saying that Jen and I are quitters, but that was our second and final attempt at making wine, because we learned some things during the process.

Number one, we didn't enjoy the process.

Number two, we weren't good at the process.

Number three, there are plenty of other people who enjoy and are good at the process.

The most important thing we produced from those grapes was awareness. Awareness that our wine-making skills are limited to tasting, appreciating and encouraging those who actually possess good wine-making skills.

So as you sow a harvest of success, Jen and I will hoist a glass of wine (made by someone else) that your bounty will be plentiful and will play to your individual strengths.

List some of your unique strengths.

Any Problems with Homosexuality?

Having an awareness of your individual strengths is a key starting point for any professional career endeavor.

Those suffering from papaphobia probably won't be bound for the altar of Catholic priesthood. Linonophobes aren't your most likely tailors, seamstresses or dominatrices. But don't go assuming that someone dealing with acrophobia can't be a pilot.

Fear of the Pope, string and heights aside, I knew I wanted a future in military service in some form or fashion. I had the desire, the citizenship and the Armed Services Vocational Aptitude Battery test scores. In high school, my community service endeavors, athletic participation and good—well, decent—grades made attendance at a military academy an option.

Applying to any military academy is exactly the bureaucratic process you would expect of a federal entity. Forms in quadruplicate, repetitive and impersonal interrogations and red tape delaying appointments up until you're least prepared and then, at which time, you are late and suddenly behind schedule.

Going through the congressional nomination process and having a congressman or senator put their name and reputation behind you only means you are cleared for the remainder of the process that verifies your academic, character, physical and medical qualities meet the academy's standards. All the reviews carefully measure each applicant's leadership potential.

The paperwork for your character assessment includes:

1. Three teacher evaluations to gain insight into your academic performance and personal character.

2. A writing sample to evaluate your aptitude for commissioned service and the coveted opportunity to show your unique experiences while demonstrating critical thinking, organizational and grammatical abilities.

3. Up to two letters of recommendation from individuals who can speak about your character, integrity, leadership abilities and experiences (hopefully in a positive light).

4. A personal data record review so you can relive your run-ins with the law, including traffic

violations, expressed both from your point of view and in the form of official court and police documentation.

5. An extracurricular composite score of school, community and work activities.

6. A drug and alcohol abuse certificate, which is just a form certifying that you don't abuse drugs and/or alcohol. I offer that explanation because at first glance it reads like a participation trophy…"Hey, I abused drugs AND alcohol today!" I imagine a little icon of a bartender giving a thumbs up in one corner and a surfer dude giving a hang loose gesture in another. The celebration of your drug and alcohol abuse also lets you know that "past experimentation with marijuana is not necessarily disqualifying," just in case you had inhalation questions. It does not, however, define the number of times after which "experimentation" becomes "regular usage."

Once you've been assessed as a character fit for the academy—and trust me, the place has some characters—you can move on to the Candidate Fitness Assessment. Your strength, agility, speed and endurance are tested with a basketball throw, pull-ups, a shuttle run, sit-ups, push-ups and a one-mile run. That series of athletic tasks helps determine whether you have the stamina to successfully complete the academy's physical program.

And your stamina is further tested by an all-day medical exam. The Department of Defense Medical Examination Review Board, acronymed DoDMERB (and pronounced *DOD-murb*) determines all service academy applicants' medical qualifications. We're talking visual acuity, refractive error, hearing, height, weight, body fat, as well as a physical inspection for tattoos and brands.

There are limits to the content of the artwork permanently injected into your skin, but each branch of service has different limitations. The Army currently doesn't limit the size or number of tattoos on your legs or arms. The Air Force has erased its previous regulation that only allowed up to 25% of any exposed body part to be covered by ink. And the Navy has altered its policies to allow sailors to sport one neck tattoo and full sleeves.

The strict military regulations on tattoos have relaxed over the years as senior leaders saw the rules costing them otherwise qualified recruits. And so, as future military members grow up in a society that is more accepting of tattoos, the military is changing their policies along with them.

And with regard to any non-visible conditions, DoDMERB mentors will advise you to "use good judgment when listing medical problems." Self-diagnosing a problem can shorten your appointment and end your path to the academy.

What I'm saying is, this is not the place to reveal that you're a hypochondriac, which ironically is a condition that would disqualify you from service. And as our understanding of psychopathology has advanced, the list of disorders that are considered truly detrimental and disqualifying has morphed over the years, but I think hypochondriasis is still on the list.

Hereditary diarrhea is no longer disqualifying since it runs in your genes. Dissociative disorder is a disqualifier because of the cost of paying multiple people in one uniform. And fortunately, Witzelsucht wasn't added until after I retired. Witzelsucht is a set of rare neurological symptoms manifest in a tendency to make puns or tell inappropriate jokes or pointless stories in socially inappropriate situations. What can I say? I was born this way.

And speaking of being born this way and inappropriate situations and disqualifying disorders, at the time I was being DoDMERBed, homosexuality was on the long list of things you couldn't be if you wanted to serve in the military or attend a service academy.

Now, I've known since I was four years old that I am gay. Sorry, was I supposed to give a "spoiler alert" warning?

While mainstream organizations no longer classified homosexuality as a mental disorder, the military still did when I was applying to the academy. So, having made it through the other wickets of the academy application process, here I am, at my physical, about to be DoDMERBed by a mousy male doctor in a lab coat and holding a clipboard (every gay girl's dream).

"Any illegal drug use?"

"No, sir." Which is a true story. I didn't even *drink* in high school.

"Any criminal record?"

"No, sir." Also a true story. When my friends hung out with me, their parents didn't give them a curfew. So, I was the furthest thing from a felon (back then).

"Any problems with homosexuality?"

Yikes.

Now, Doctor Mouse didn't ask if I *am* homosexual, he asked if I had any problems with it. So, since I haven't officially been diagnosed with this rare condition and not wanting to volunteer any other information, I answer the question I am asked.

"No, sir." Again, true story. I have no problems with it. In fact, I'm actually quite good at it.

This is also when I realize I am more than a label. Whether I am categorized as brunette, female, Asian, youngest child or gay, I have a contribution to make as a public servant and as a military leader. This has helped me see past other people's labels, because we're all more than just bins of gender, ethnicity, orientation, birth order or hair color.

Fortunately, a few years into my career, homosexuality would come out of the list of prohibited activities. I ended up retiring from the Air Force with a spouse who is a blonde, female, Caucasian and an oldest child. And gay.

List all the different labels that define you.

Venting in the Bathroom

Regardless of the labels that we can adorn in life, one equalizing label at U.S. military academies is "freshman." Freshman year at the Air Force Academy is a unique experience. Not just in the sense that it's a rare event that only 1,100 young people engage in each year, but also in the sense that it's an unconventional first year at college.

There are 40 cadet squadrons with about 25 cadets per class, per squadron. That's not the odd part—keep reading. The two rectangular academy dorm buildings housing the cadet wing are laid out so that two squadrons share a square floor plan, each squadron getting one *L*-shaped half. Still not odd yet, I know. Stop interrupting.

While upperclassmen are allowed to travel freely between squadrons, freshmen cadets are not. In fact, while penned in by invisible lines of squadron demarcation, freshmen cadets must travel the hallways of their assigned squadron *L* by walking in a strict position of attention along the right wall. All turns must be 90-degree facing movements. If you're thinking of robots, you're visualizing the gait accurately. And this manner of traversing through the dorms (and around the entire campus, actually) is the normal deployment of travel. Well, normal if you're in your first year at the Air Force Academy. So that's the odd part. That, and we aren't allowed to talk in the hallways. Talking robots would be absurd.

We may be odd robots, but we've got the intelligence to figure out a way to overcome the artificial boundaries separating us from other first-year robots. One of those ways is meeting up for stealthy conversations in the bathrooms located on opposite corners where the Ls come together to create a square. Since rank has its privilege and very few people seek out accommodations near restrooms, freshmen rooms are typically the dorm rooms that share a wall with the corner bathrooms. But this only facilitates our plan for surreptitious conversation dominion…those higher-ranking cadets fall right into our trap.

Not only do the rooms share a wall with the bathroom, they share an air register. It's not as gross as it sounds. Scents don't travel through the bathroom–dorm room register, but sounds do (please note the restraint employed to not make a doo pun). The corner dorm room becomes the de facto hub of message relay between freshmen cadets on that floor.

Whenever we want to chat with a freshman from the neighboring squadron, we go to the bathroom and knock on the register until one of the room's operators comes online. Then we either vent through the register with whomever answers, relay a message through the ducting or beckon someone to the bathroom. The steps are manifold.

Tonight, weighed down by insomnia and an intensive academic load, I ambulate myself to the bathroom, squaring my corners and dragging my right shoulder along walls even though no one is awake, much less out in the halls to monitor me. We've been programmed well.

I knock on the register with a high degree of confidence that my classmates are also awake. We're like the fairytale elves, treading around only at night, just not as productive and certainly not sewing our souls for upperclass cobblers. After a quick chat through the metal channel, two of my classmates right-face into the bathroom. In there, we catch up, gripe and laugh, all at the volume of a grounded hummingbird's wings.

After a healthy verbal expulsion of all the discomforts of freshman cadet life, we disband our klatsch and bid each other bidet (bet you wish I'd played that doo pun earlier now, don't ya?). Like the obedient automaton that I am, I square my corner as I depart the bathroom. I didn't go in there for any physiological relief, but hanging out with co-commiseraters brings me psychological relief. That relief cushions the shock of seeing one of the squadron's seniors when I get out into the hallway.

Accompanying the shock of seeing any non-freshman out at this hour is the confusion of how to mandatorily greet her. The typical action when a freshman passes any upperclassman is to loudly shout a standard greeting of, "GOOD [morning, afternoon, evening] CADET [so and so]." Midnight is that magical tipping point well beyond evening and too premature for morning, so I'm not sure which salutation to choose from the menu. Also at odds with normal is the hall volume setting. As tempting as it is to yell a greeting, any greeting, at the top of my lungs, I know the wrath that would ensue, so I opt for a respectful hushed, "Good evening, Cadet De Freitas."

"Barrett," she softly calls, preempting the wrath of waking anyone from their slumber. The volume of her tone of voice indicates she's not just responding to my restrained greeting; there's a follow-up conversation to be had.

"Yes, ma'am?" I stop, execute a flawless 90-degree turn to face her and stand at a rigid position of attention. It may be the middle of the night, but military decorum is 24/7.

Air Force Academy protocol would also permit this senior cadet to demand a verbatim recitation of any number of facts, figures or quotes we are required to memorize. She can demand to know Major General John M. Schofield's graduation address to the graduating class of 1879 at West Point. By the way, that's the 16-word (or 15 and an initial) preface anytime we recite the quote. Word for word. Oh and, 32 years later, hearing just the name "Schofield" triggers all 16 of those words, in that order, to come to my brain. Every. Single. Time.

So, I'm ready to tell her that the discipline that makes the soldiers of a free country reliable in battle is not to be gained by harsh or tyrannical treatment. On the contrary, (if you know the quote, that's a funny transition) her request is a more personal one.

"Barrett, did you have fun talking in the bathroom?" Her quiet accusation has the soft edges of a caring mother who guides you to realize your own bad decisions without ever having to raise her voice. The kind of gentle nurturing that makes you feel worse than if someone were just in your face shouting spittle through syllables.

Well, crap. (What's with the poo puns? Was that my first one? Or was that number two?) Her question doesn't leave me much maneuver room. I mean, I can deny and therefore imply she's a liar for thinking I had been talking in the bathroom. But it seems she already knows of my bathroom talking infraction, so I admit to the crime.

"Yes, ma'am," I whisper.

"Don't do it again."

"Yes, ma'am."

"Go to bed."

"Yes, ma'am."

And with that, Cadet De Freitas releases me. I pivot on my outside foot to turn toward my room, unsure if I have just been reprimanded for talking in the bathroom or praised for coming clean.

Either way, it's another valuable lesson I learn in the *L*-shaped hallways of the Air Force Academy dorms. Cadet De Freitas didn't belittle me and didn't give me a chance to get myself caught up in a lie, but she did make me aware that I didn't get away with anything.

Yet another memory that reminds me I had an *L* of a time there.

Who is someone in your life who modeled positive leadership?

Flashlight

I think part of the reason Cadet De Freitas didn't give me a chance to lie and went right to assuming that I had been talking in the bathroom is because we had a little bit of a history.

During basic cadet training, also known as "Beast," the restrictions on first-year cadets are even tighter than they are during the academic year. During the academic year, taps sounds over the campus-wide giant voice at 2300 (11 pm), but most freshmen are still up working on the heavy academic load we carry. Taps means lights out and you better be in bed by the 24th note of the bugle solo.

Because we are still in civilian to military transition during Beast, we have a little more supervision. Soon after the bugler puts away his instrument, upperclassmen, also known as "Beast Masters," go around to each basic cadet's room for dormitory inspection, aka DI, because it's the military and everything must be able to be reduced to an acronym.

I think legally they're checking for the correct number of basic cadets in each room, but the real thrill for the Beast Masters is in catching any number of basic cadets doing stupid stuff in their room. And because the Air Force Academy isn't like most other colleges, "stupid stuff" is all relative.

Like tonight, the stupid stuff I'm doing is strobing my issued flashlight across the dormitory quad and into another basic cadets' room. In a rare moment when we are allowed to converse freely with our classmates, we have coordinated the signal, which when mirrored back means "head to the corner bathroom for some illicit chatter."

Again, because the Air Force Academy isn't like most other colleges, "illicit chatter" doesn't mean anything dirty; it just means talking when we aren't otherwise allowed to.

My roommate, unamused by illicit chatter and possibly hurt that her chatter isn't illicit enough for me, is already fast asleep in her bunk. So it's just me, standing at the window, stupidly flashing a flashlight across the quad, waiting for the reciprocal signal so I know to head to the bathroom.

No return light.

I double-check my flashlight and confirm it's functioning properly. I flick the switch back and forth for another round of illegible morse code.

No return light.

Having proved my persistent nature in just getting in to the Air Force Academy, I refuse to give up on this process either.

I narrow the focus of the beam coming out of my flashlight, take more precise aim at my friends' window and project the signal once again.

Then I see it! A flood of return light.

Except it's not coming from the flashlight of a friend across the quad. It's coming from the reflection of hall light through our door, thrown open by the foe of a Beast Master.

There stands Cadet De Freitas. And because this is the first time I've done something stupid, correction, because this is the first time she's caught me doing something stupid, she asks (loudly), "BARRETT! What are you doing?"

I am still in that civilian to military transition, so I'm not entirely well-versed in the exact way to respond, except I know there's a "ma'am" involved.

So, standing there with my flashlight still on and still pointing across the quad, I say, "Ma'am! Nothing!" which clearly is not the case and we all know it. Cadet De Freitas doesn't even humor that statement with a response and instead stands there with a hand on her hip in a stance that means "this is not going to end well for you" in civilian or military parlance.

And it doesn't.

"Submarine," Cadet De Freitas orders.

It may seem like a bizarre issuance for a school that isn't nautically based, but as I've said, the Air Force Academy isn't like most other colleges, and "submarine" is more verb than noun here.

Leaving my flashlight by the window (and probably still on), I ascend the ladder to my bunk. I submerge headfirst under the wool blanket and top sheet of my perfectly made bed.

"Ten!" Cadet De Freitas issues the sentence of my punishment. And I begin the execution of 10 push-ups under the cover and top sheet of my bed.

It may not seem like much of a punishment, but since most basic cadets don't sleep under their covers, it is a hefty sanction. Especially when there are anywhere between 70 to 5,000 safety pins stuck through the sheet and blanket on our bed, securing hospital corners to the mattress to ensure the bed is tight enough to bounce a ROLL of quarters off of it.

In fact, if Cadet De Freitas would look more closely at my sleeping roommate, she'd see that she is lying corpse-like on top of her perfectly made bed. But Cadet De Freitas is only watching me carry out my sentence. Watching…and listening, as anywhere between 70 to 5,000 safety pins loudly pop out of their punctured position with each push-up.

I resurface after completing my submarines and get into a position of attention for any further punishment, aside from the sleep I'll now lose having to re-pin my bed (after Cadet De Freitas leaves).

Silently, I stare at Cadet De Freitas, waiting as she thinks of the next cruel, punitive action.

I see an inspired idea illuminate her face, then fade.

The radiance of another revelation reflects off her face, then fades.

The shine of a third suggestion strikes, then fades.

Cadet De Freitas pushes past me to our window, counts the windows to identify the room of my friends who are now flashing their lights to beckon me to the bathroom.

"Barrett, go to bed," she orders as she leaves my room to impose the same submarine sentence on my friends.

"Yes, ma'am," I whisper back, still standing at attention. Until Cadet De Freitas shuts the door.

I scurry back to the window and frantically flash a steady beam of light in a circular motion, our prearranged signal for calling it off, whatever "it" was. They repeated the circular pattern with their flashlight and then both our lights went dark. I knew that they had received the message.

I was happy to take the heat for my basic cadet buddies. I would have to spend a significant hour or so remaking my bed, but they shouldn't have to as well.

My dorm room door flies open again. De Freitas. "Barrett. Go to bed. I mean it."

"Yes, ma'am."

And I did.

Right after I re-pinned my bed.

Name a time you "took one for the team."

Slow Swimming, That's My Jam

Signaling a flashlight in a circular warning motion wasn't the first time I realized how important it was to be a good, supportive teammate. Whether it was soccer, basketball, doubles tennis, couples beer pong or swimming, I always preferred group effort over solo performance.

Quick flashback to a time when I looked a heck of a lot better in a swimsuit. I'm a competitive member of a relay swim team. We're in the throes of a meet, and our pool's reputation is on the line. I'm the second swimmer on our medley relay because, well, I can't do the butterfly stroke, the anchor position is too much pressure for me and quite frankly, the breaststroke leg is reserved for the slowest swimmer. And slow swimming, that's my jam.

Our starting swimmer is the region's speed backstroker, so we have a comfortable lead by the time I splash in for my leg. I maintain our team's lead, but second and third places are breathing down our necks...or splashing down our suits (I don't know what the metaphor is).

By the time our anchor man (not to be confused with Ron Burgundy) gets in the pool, our lead is very, very narrow. With each freestyle stroke, our margin of victory is decreasing. The swimmers seem to collectively decide to create a photo finish suitable for a made-for-TV documentary. They are neck and neck…or goggle and goggle (again, I'm unsure of the metaphor, but I feel like I'm drowning in my attempts…there, I know that metaphor will float).

When our teammate finally touches the wall, the cheers are deafening.

But the cheers are not for us.

The lead we had maintained for three legs was lost in the fourth.

Our anchor swimmer knows the lead was lost on her watch, and she is devastated. She starts bawling because of the responsibility she bears for this blemish on our record. I stand there with her as she sobs, while our two relay mates make their way to our side of the pool.

Swimming is typically an individual sport, but when it's a relay race, all of a sudden it's a team sport. When one individual on the team is the one who loses the lead, all of a sudden the team sport is once again an individual sport. So assigning blame is a tough call. Our team captain, however, is up to the challenge of making that tough decision. So when our team captain gets over to me and Anchor, she really leans into her—meaning, she reads her the riot act.

I thought Anchor couldn't cry any harder, but Captain makes that very impossible task possible. Yelling at Anchor for losing the lead. Screaming at her for being slow. Calling her freestyle stroke a crawl (which is *technically* what the stroke is called, so burn on Captain).

I feel helpless.

It's obvious that Anchor knows the lead was lost during her leg. But the argument could also be made that we all contributed to the loss. If we had ALL swam just a little bit faster, we would have reduced the pressure to gain back any of that loss during the last leg. And I was pretty sure Anchor didn't meticulously and maliciously calculate her stroke rate to purposely lose the race.

So I decide to lean into her too. But, I wanted to accentuate the positive. I needed to give her something to cushion the blow that Captain was dealing. I wrapped my arm around Anchor, sucked in a voluminous intake of air, worthy of the compliment I was about to bestow upon her and said, "You breathed really well."

It was the best I could come up with.

It was actually <u>all</u> I could come up with.

I mean, I was only eight years old and this was a community pool swim team.

The memory of that day reminds me that every team event requires individual participation, and everyone's individual participation contributes to a larger team.

It's easy to pick apart other people for their negative contributions. It takes some splashing around to find a positive.

Keep swimming for those positives, and if all else fails, feel free to use, "You breathed really well."

What's the most unusual encouragement you've ever received?

Your Kid Throws Like a Girl

I don't know that biologists have sequenced DNA for a sportsmanship gene, but based on the pride my parents have for my sportsmanship trophies, it might be less nature and more nurture. My parents were always prouder if I won a sportsmanship award than if I had earned "highest scorer" or "best rebounder."

I had a *Brady Bunch*-meets-*Mr. Mom* sort of upbringing, not in a scene-by-scene recreation kind of way but in a widowed father brings in kids to a new marriage and becomes a stay-at-home-dad kind of way.

My dad was significantly older than my mom (and me), so my childhood was Mom working and Dad making my lunch and taking me to school. Each evening, Dad and I would walk down the street where Mom's work carpool dropped her off. While we waited, we would stand on opposite sides of the street and play some sort of kick or catch. One evening we might be pushing a soccer ball from foot to foot. The next we might be wielding baseball mitts, pretending we were Major League Baseball outfielders warming up in between innings.

Dad brought two boys and three girls into his marriage to my mom. I'm not sure if he wanted gender symmetry, but from the birth announcement he drafted days before my arrival to the improvised pink bows taped to my bald baby head, the consensus was that I would be, or was, a boy. Even Mom's doctor told her she was either having a boy or a tom girl.

Tonight, Dad and his tom girl daughter are playing catch with a football.

As we toss the pigskin back and forth, a neighbor jokingly (I think...I hope) yells out, "Hey Wally! Your kid throws like a girl!"

Dad laughed and yelled back, "That's funny, Ted!"

As soon as we see Ted head back into his house, Dad audibles a father-daughter huddle, "Get! Over! Here!"

To this day, I don't know if his reaction was embarrassment, because I <u>did</u> throw like a girl, or benevolence, because he wanted to teach his daughter to <u>not</u> throw like a girl.

But there on the carpool drop-off spot, he teaches me the basics of throwing a perfect spiral. I never got the chance to throw (or catch) a perfect (or imperfect) spiral on the gridiron, but at least Dad knew I could.

And we never heard any complaints from Ted again.

What gender (or other) stereotypes have you encountered?

He Cheered Me On

Some evenings, when we knew Ted wasn't home or judging my dad's daughter's football arm, Dad and I would bounce a basketball across the street or pretend to shoot an imaginary free throw (it was a National Basketball Association regulation-width street).

I was able to put our basketball drills to good use on an official organized basketball team, but not as organized and official as the NBA or WNBA. And to prevent any grievances from Ted about my basketball shooting form (God forbid I shoot like a girl), my parents sprung for me to attend a summer basketball camp.

My conflict-averse nature in life also rears its peaceful head in my athletic endeavors; I play defensive positions in soccer, would rather rebound than shoot in basketball and play the coveted "left out" in softball, as in second-string bench. In the only sort of conversion therapy I'm a fan of, the basketball camp focuses on rebounds as a way of getting the ball in my hands so I can put the ball in the basket without passing it off to a teammate for their glory moment.

Dad stands on the sidelines with other parents during basketball camp, not because he's a coach but because he's a supportive Dad (and retired...and social...and possibly bored). Of course, just as in the Mr. Mom plotline, Dad is amongst mostly moms, and as Dad's a little bit of a flirt, I think his attendance at basketball camp is more than just a chauffeuring responsibility for him. Nothing offensive of course.

Look at me being all defensive of my dad.

Speaking of offense and defense, on the basketball court, my play doesn't have a cute moniker or clever name; it could have been called exactly what it was—"get the ball to Michelle so she can shoot and hopefully score." With the ball in my hands, I look up to gauge the distance to the basket, wondering if I can just Hail Mary a perfect spiral from where I stand. The basket I'm eyeing is too far even for my advanced athletic arm, so I start dribbling (the ball—nothing about scoring makes me salivate).

Time marches in half time as I coordinate my ball bouncing with my steps. Turns out I'm just slowly trotting the forced trek to the basket. Realizing that getting this over with is in my best interest, I pick up my pace. The volume of cheers increases as my distance to the basket decreases. The loudest voice of all is my dad's. I zero in on his vocal support, surprised he is able to be drawn away from the Mr. Mom equivalent of playing coupon poker with the moms on the sideline. Once hand-feet coordination is in swing, I'm able to keep my head up and my eyes trained on my destination. Tunnel vision boxes out everything else, including any opposition.

The louder the yells become, the more I train my ears on Dad's voice. I'm about to score my first two points in basketball, and my dad is there to witness it. Even Ted would be proud about this.

In gangly form, I throw the ball from my hands and the backboard courts it to the rim where the net embraces it to secure my first score in a new sport.

Just as surprised as everyone else, I turn to get a high five, chest bump or even an appropriate good game from a teammate, coach or the referee, but no one is near me. I had outrun the opposition and my team stood in awe of the fact that I had finally put a ball in the basket.

I turned to the scoreboard to watch my two-point contribution get added to my team. But the only numerical movement happens on the opposing team's side of the board.

It turns out that the opposition didn't chase me because I was running toward their basket.

And the awe from my team was rooted in the fact that, after all this time trying to get me to score, I scored for the wrong team.

Whether Dad knew or cared about which basket belonged to my team, all I remember is that he cheered me on the entire time.

Who are your true supporters in life (the ones who would cheer you on even if you were aiming for the wrong basket)?

Let It Go! Let It Go!

Sometimes I think my dad was such a vocal supporter of my illustrious display of basketball court spatial awareness because there was a time when his cheers weren't so supportive.

Mom, Dad, my older brother Earl and I are taking advantage of idyllic spring weather on the grounds of a local park. In addition to devouring a homemade picnic lunch, today's agenda includes teaching me to fly a kite. At the advanced age of five, this is my first time flying a kite—a sure sign of having led an obviously deprived childhood.

With bellies full of Mom's cooking and baking, kite pilot ground school begins. Earl stands down-string while my small hands cradle the spool, waiting for the commands from instructor Dad. It seems that Dad's ability to provide thorough instructions is blocked by his visions of being featured in a Norman Rockwell graphic as the next cover of the *Saturday Evening Post* with a depiction of the little Mrs. on a picnic blanket adoringly watching her husband's prowess as a father as he flies a kite with their young son and daughter.

Cherry blossom petals flutter by, giving Norman some painting reprieve as Dad uses the petals as a windsock letting him know we are a go for sending his parenting artistry aloft. Unsure of when the next breeze might be, Dad skips the preflight brief usually involved in ground school and we fly ahead to the takeoff. The line between my spool of string and the kite in Earl's hands is now taut as Earl waits for the launch sequence to begin.

I know now, applying lessons from several college aerodynamics classes and actual pilot ground school, that kite flight is controlled by lift, gravity and drag. The lifting force of the wind overcomes the downward pull of gravity and the drag of air resistance. The small amount of tension on the line allows the kite to rise effortlessly upward. As the breeze evolves into a gust, that small amount of tension increases into a large amount of straight-line force…enough to torque the arms of a five-year-old girl.

Dad's excitement also increases as the impending kite launch brings definition to the *Saturday Evening Post* cover drawing. He sees the resistance in the kite-line between me and Earl and in the arm-line between me and the spool. And from the kite launch control center of his mind, he starts barking out commands.

Had I not skipped ground school, I might have understood the action required of the commands.

Had I flown a kite before, I might have understood the intent of the commands.

Had I been older than five, I might have been a more independent-thinking student.

But, as a five-year-old first-time kite flyer who never went to ground school, I take Dad's commands literally. I say "commands" but there is really only one command that Dad issues and that is, "Let it go!" It just seems like multiple commands because he says it repeatedly.

The command is for Earl and me, and Earl obediently lets it—the kite—go.

Had I not skipped ground school, I might have understood "let it go" means to release some of the line from the spool.

Had I flown a kite before, I might have understood the intent of "let it go" means releasing enough line to allow the aerodynamic structure of the kite to gain lift from the wind.

Had I been older than five, I might have understood "let it go" does <u>not</u> mean let go of the entire spool of string once cradled in my small hands.

Like Earl, I obediently let it—the entire spool of string—go.

And go it does.

The string once stretched between me and Earl, tethering the kite to the ground, is now merely an additional tail doing little to assist the real tail in keeping the kite's nose up and balanced. The tether-turned-tail grows longer, and the spool of extra tether grows smaller as the gust-turned-sustained-high-wind pulls more string from the spool. The spool of string continues to fuel the wind's demands, hijacking the kite's flight.

Unaware that this isn't kite flying, I stare skyward as the colorful diamond shape disappears into the heavens. It seems a bit anticlimactic, but I'm five, what do I know?

Life back down on earth quickly becomes hell for five-year-old me for sacrificing a kite with my direct disobedience of Dad. Hell for five-year-old me is having my dad yell at me, "WHAT ARE YOU DOING? WHY DID YOU LET IT GO? WHAT ARE YOU THINKING?"

I would have answered, "Flying a kite. Because you said to." And "I'm thinking this isn't how you fly a kite."

However, that response is obstructed by the word, "WAAAAAAAAAAHHHHHHHHH" and accompanied by tears. Lots of tears.

Dad doesn't understand where the breakdown in communication is, because he knows what "let it go" means. I don't understand the yelling, because I'm old enough to know what "let it go" means.

We don't have time to bicker over intention and interpretation because we have a kite to catch. Brother Earl is on it, so Dad continues to loudly explain what "let it go" means to him.

Actually, I say "explain" but there is really only one explanation that Dad uses and that is, "Let it go!" It's like looking up a word in the dictionary, only to find the word you're looking up is used in the definition of the word you're looking up. So for now, I just let it— my tears—go.

My tears modify Rockwell's cover drawing to that of a mother laughing at the sight of her well-meaning, poorly executing husband yelling at their tearful youngest while an older son sprints after a dwindling spool of string across the picturesque lawn of a county park.

Actually, the image worthy of Norman Rockwell's utensils is the resolution of the kite-losing, Dad-yelling exhibition, a depiction of a father and daughter in a loving and apologetic embrace with the little Mrs. on a picnic blanket adoringly watching her husband's prowess as a father as the tiny speck of a kite disappears high over the head of their son.

Sometimes, in the heat of the kite, we get tethered to the intention of our words without realizing there might be another possible interpretation. When the miscommunication is identified, it's best to just let it go and start over.

That's just the way the kite flies.

Have you ever miscommunicated in the heat of a moment?

Somewhere Between a Bird and a Rock

One thing worth noting about a kite successfully in flight is that its angle with respect to the horizon puts the kite in a perpetual stall. A stall might keep a kite airborne, but a stall in other airborne crafts, like an airplane, is not considered part of successful flight.

I learned this very fact the summer after my freshman year at the Air Force Academy. As part of the first-summer curriculum, you either jump out of perfectly good airplanes or learn to fly airplanes. Being of sound mind, I choose the stay-in-the-plane option.

Today's agenda includes a "confidence maneuver" of stalling the aircraft, which means we're gonna starve the plane of airspeed by disrupting the airflow under the wing that normally keeps the plane aloft. This asinine maneuver is designed to teach me to recognize and prevent a stall from happening or to recover from a stall if I fail to recognize and prevent it from happening.

Out in a motorized glider, the guy next to me is an Air Force instructor pilot (read: full-on grown-up) stuck flying with a college kid (read: me) who thinks she's all that just because she made it through her first year at the Air Force Academy.

He points the nose of the aircraft to the sky, pulls back on the throttle...and we wait. Soon the aircraft loses its upward momentum, and the stick between my instructor's legs becomes ineffective. Let me rephrase... the mechanism that controls the surfaces on the aircraft becomes ineffective.

The plane starts shaking. We're at that wonderful moment between flying and falling. That wonderful moment between being a bird and a rock.

And now, according to my instructor's pre-brief, the plane will start looking for a flying attitude. Because the plane "wants to fly," it will seek airspeed, and the fastest way to do that is to drop its nose over. So I am fully expecting the plane to go from nose high to nose low, just like my instructor said it would.

Today, the plane goes from nose high to...*right* wing low.

To my left, I see only sky.

To my right, I see only ground. Fast-approaching ground.

The first step of the stall recovery is to push the nose of the aircraft straight down, so what was once sky-earth is now all-earth. And my instructor executes the steps of the stall recovery like it's the most boring task in the world.

He is unconcerned that we are nose-diving toward our death. One hand on the throttle, the other on the stick (that once ineffective thing between his legs is becoming useful).

After what feels like an hour of plummeting toward terra firma, the plane is finally flying straight and level and my heart rate slows down double the triple digits.

The cockpit is quiet, aside from my panting.

My instructor breaks the solitude by asking if I'm ok.

What a stupid question! We just survived an almost certain death experience together!

I bluff, "Yea."

"You sure?"

"YEA." No manners, no military decorum, just a snotty retort from a kid who still thinks she's the bomb because she's made it through her first year at the Air Force Academy. I seem to have forgotten that I am the lowest-ranking person at a military institution talking with an officer who's been through a commissioning program, pilot training and years of military service that have warranted a "sir" prefix or suffix to every phrase that comes out of my mouth.

"Ok." My instructor seems to let that breach slide and also seems to buy that I'm actually ok (because I'm not).

My play-it-cool victory is short-lasting.

As it turns out, at some point during the stall or stall recovery, for whatever reason—maybe it was instinct, reaction or foreplay—I grabbed my instructor's leg. And unaware that I had put my hand there, I am equally unaware that it is still there.

All the "sirs" that I left out before came gushing out in between "Oh my Gods" and "I'm sorrys." I quickly retract my hand to my side of the cockpit.

Fast-forward a couple years. Now it's the summer after my junior year at the Academy and I'm learning to fly the Cessna 172. Again on the agenda is the ridiculous let-the-plane-fall-out-of-the-sky maneuver.

Same setup as before. Instructor pilot to my right, stuck flying with a college kid who knows she's all that because she made it through three years at the Academy. Nose to the sky, back on the throttle, lose momentum, ineffective stick between legs, plane shakes, bird, rock, looking for flight.

But, I've been through this before. I know to be ready for nose high to nose low or nose high to right wing low. I've even been through left wing low. And today the plane goes nose low, the instructor aggressively executes the recovery and I keep my hands to myself.

But my instructor is demonstrating something completely new: secondary stalls, which is what happens when you do an aggressive stall recovery, like the one he did. So we go nose high, nose low, hands to self, pass through straight and level and back to…

Nose up, no momentum, useless stick, shaking plane, bird, rock, aaaaannnnnndddddd, right wing low.

This time—call it natural reaction, call it automated response or keep calling it foreplay—I once again grab my instructor's leg. This, of course, is how rumors start and reputations are built. However, this is not the reputation I'm trying to establish, so I once again retract my hand to my side of the cockpit.

Fast-forward a couple more years. I'm in pilot training, heading out to stall the T-37. You know the drill…nose up, no momentum, penis innuendo, shaking plane, bird, rock aaaaaand looking for flight.

But my instructor is demonstrating yet another new confidence maneuver: unloaded recoveries, which means the plane will find its flying attitude wherever it damn well pleases, which today, is behind us. So we start an unexpected, lazy float backwards and upside down. And because it was unexpected, what do you think I did? Spoiler alert: I grabbed his leg.

It may be surprising that I ended up in a crew aircraft, since flying a single-seat plane would have been a wiser choice as far as inappropriate airborne touching goes.

My leg-gripping evolution spanned five years, three different airframes and three separate instructors. To become a pilot, I had to let go of my instructors' legs, leverage the lessons from the new environment of the last iteration and prove I could execute recoveries on my own.

For the sake of complete reporting, I'll say that I did make it through the different flying programs.

For the sake of honest reporting, I'll say that during follow on stalls and stall recovery demonstrations, I did *want* to grab someone's leg but I learned to let it be my own.

And, eventually, my hands were on the controls because, as part of the program, I had to be the one putting the plane into a stall and executing the recovery. And that took both of my hands.

For many of the new skills we learn, we initially lean on (or in my case, grope) mentors as we learn new skills in ever-changing environments. Each experience teaches us valuable insights that can be applied to the next time, providing skills that can be applied to the next time (and so on and so on).

Every single one of us is going through new experiences in the midst of constantly changing environments. End results may be similar, but each time will teach you something that you can layer onto future decisions.

It's ok to lean on others at first, but at some point, we need to get our hands on the controls and fly our own plane, because when we grip too hard, we stall our life.

What skill did you once need to lean on someone for that you can now do by yourself?

May's Not Here

Laughter and levity are the legs I grab when I feel my life start to stall. That's why I preach "Laugh, Learn, Think" (in that order) as my life and business motivation.

I always wanted to write a book called "Laughing at Alzheimer's." Not because I think there's anything funny about Alzheimer's disease, but because humor was the main way my family dealt with the evil theft of my dad's wit, intelligence, dignity, independence and personality.

My mom still has a note she wrote capturing one of Dad's lucid moments during his eight-year campaign against dementia. It was early on in the war and in what must have been an infuriating conflict between the clarity of an educated man and the vacant vault of a once abundant brain.

Dad looked at us, and his eyes sharpened, announcing the arrival of a rare moment of clarity. "May," he demanded of my mom, "I wanna know who's in charge of making me crazy!" Then, immediately after his inquiry, Alzheimer's stole my dad back to its thieving grips.

Mom and I just laughed. What else could we do?

We couldn't answer his question because we had the exact same concern. And while we were active in the Alzheimer's Association, at home, alone with the burgling effects of a terrible disease, laughter was the primary caregiver for us as caregivers.

As Dad's condition worsened, he "graduated" out of adult caregiving services, confined to his home, just as his once vibrant mind was imprisoned in his skull. The family took turns helping Mom, giving her a break from the strain of feeding, changing, bathing and medicating her husband, our dad.

Tonight, after an evening of singing patriotic tunes with a man who could remember every single lyric but had no recollection of me, my name or the fact that we are related, I get ready for the physically demanding task of getting Dad into bed.

The transfer from wheelchair to bed starts with a hug. Aside from the benefit of physical connection, the hug is how I get my legs alternating with Dad's. This allows for a broader base for the following steps.

With my left leg to the outside of Dad's right side and my right leg between his legs, I raise him up as we hug, getting us both to our feet. Correction: getting us both to <u>my</u> feet.

As soon as I lift Dad up, he clamps his legs around mine. Holding up someone who outweighs you isn't an easy task, but unexpectedly holding up someone somehow makes that weight heavier.

Because he is rapidly slipping through my hug and I don't want to sit him back down and repeat any of this, I choose to leverage the death grip he has on my legs. I move on to the next step, which is getting his butt on to the bed. His grip on my legs isn't loosening, so I fast-forward to the next step of rotating him to lie on his back.

For any Ultimate Fighting Championship fans, allow me to commentate: I do a double-leg takedown and guard pass for side control. Translation: anchoring my left leg on the ground, I end up with my torso parallel to Dad's, lying across him at a diagonal.

Now we're rooted in the ground game (the bed being the ground) and, if I'm gonna win this match, I need to maintain the dominant position in the hopes of a submission by Dad. None of these words or images are words or images I really want associated with a hug between me and my dad, but what else can I do?

Dad and I are partly horizontal, and I need to get his legs onto the bed, which I typically do by gently cradling his calves in my arms to spin his legs. But with

Dad grapevining my legs, I'm forced to guard pass to full mount in the hopes that Dad will tap out or the referee will call the match on account of inappropriate metaphors.

My arms still firmly around Dad in a hug and only my left leg planted, I swing my right leg, intertwined with Dad's legs onto the bed. Dad's not going to bed without a fight, and not only do his legs stay wrapped around mine, he tightens their grip.

So now the only contact I have with the ground is my left leg. The rest of me…is in full contact with my dad… horizontally…on my parents' bed.

And Dad isn't letting go.

"Dad! Let go!"

"It's ok!"

"No, Dad, it's not. This is inappropriate!"

"Inappropriate?"

"Yes, Dad, this is inappropriate."

"May's not here." (She is.)

"THAT'S NOT WHY THIS IS INAPPROPRIATE! I'm your daughter!"

"Oh."

Quickly, I am out of Dad's embrace and I am no longer on top of my dad...in my parents' bed...in front of my mom.

Mom and I just laughed. What else could we do?

What's a time when humor helped you through an awkward or painful experience?

Does This Look Like the Casket Walter Is In?

The day after my dad passed, Jen accompanied Mom, my sisters and me as we started the emotional process of picking out a casket and a gravesite and setting a date for the viewing and funeral.

At the funeral home in the casket showroom, Jen stands patiently as we spend no less than 45 minutes discussing the merits of the casket we have all but financially committed to getting for Dad. It has a blue lining, which we like because it represents his service in the Army Air Corps and the Air Force. The lining's cross-shaped fold serves as the extra sign of God's blessing in Dad's final resting bed.

Two days later, my whole family is back at the funeral home to see Dad in his casket. In a scene sponsored by Kleenex, we're escorted to our own room where Dad lies in his flag-draped casket. Mom and my older siblings approach Dad first.

I stare at the back of their heads, waiting for my turn to pay my respects. Oddly enough, Jen, who is shorter than me, can apparently see Dad. I'm not sure what she sees but she doesn't like it. She turns to our funeral director, who is so young I suspect mommy and daddy drive him to work every day.

"Come with me," Jen barks in a very hushed voice. And away she goes.

You don't have to know Jen well to know that the only response to that particular "come with me" is to follow. And our prepubescent funeral director does exactly that.

I *do* know Jen well and, fearful for the funeral director's short life, I follow him.

Jen makes a very direct path to the casket salesroom floor and walks up to the one where she had watched us spend nearly an hour. Each casket has a professional foam core board Velcroed to the lining, spelling out the specifications of the casket, perhaps indicating which rainforest tree provided the rare wood for the overpriced box.

Jen rips the board from our casket model and thrusts it into the child's face and says, "Does this look like the casket Walter is in?"

The question appears to be rhetorical and the answer seems obvious, but the toddler funeral director feels compelled to respond. However, all that comes out are stutters, vowels and excess air.

Jen, the master of all-caps, answers her own questions and cuts him off, "NO! This one is blue." She points to the model casket lining, indicating that the sky-colored fabric is indeed what the rest of us call "blue."

"*That* casket," pointing in the direction we sort of came from—I don't think navigational accuracy is the point— "is cream colored," she says.

"*This* lining makes a cross," Jen continues. "*That* casket does not. So, I ask you again…" (man, I don't think funeral homes are supposed to be this much fun) "Does this. Look like. The casket. Walter. Is. In?"

The infant is out of words (and vowels and excess air) and Jen is out of patience. She hands the baby the foam core board and heads back to the viewing room.

Having never uttered a word, I just follow. Jen slides back into the room to pay her respects to Dad, our departure not even a blip on the rest of the family's radar. They probably don't notice our departure because they are all huddled around Dad's casket…hovering is more like it…inappropriately hovering over Dad.

In a classic divide and conquer maneuver, while Jen and I were undertaking the case of the mixed-up casket, the rest of my family identified some things about Dad's look that they don't like. So when Jen and I get back to the viewing room, my family rapid fires the list of grievances to me.

Dad's lips are too pale, his eyebrows aren't brushed and there's makeup on his bright white sideburns. The three-shot machine gun bursts of complaints make the three items seem like 6, or 9, or 12...anything divisible by three.

As I take the volley of dissatisfaction, Jen turns to our funeral director, still in his foxhole from the casket battle. Her glare hits its target, and the funeral director crawls as far from Jen as the small room permits.

As the only seemingly objective person in the room, Jen is appointed as the delegate to follow up in two days for all things needing to be fixed.

The funeral director's entire body collapses at the thought of having to deal with Jen again as mine inflates with anticipation of being the lucky spectator at what will surely be another fun round of Jen versus the funeral director.

List some of the people who stand up for you and your loved ones.

Jewish Carpenter

Jen and I are en route to see her new BFF, the funeral director, to see if he's fixed the mistakes made on Dad's burial prep makeup. Unable to drive in silence, I hear Jen ask, "What's so funny about a Jewish carpenter?"

"What are you talking about?" Although I'm not sure why I ask, this is a normal course of conversation for Jen and me (and why I try to nap while she drives).

"I don't get this bumper sticker."

I don't want to look up. I'm working on a funeral photo slideshow on my laptop while sitting shotgun and still mourning. But, I look up. All I see is that we are just another car in a line of many, waiting impatiently for a stoplight to turn green.

"What bumper sticker is confusing you?" I ask her frustratedly.

Jen points to the one on the car directly in front of us. *My boss is a Jewish carpenter.*

"Are you serious?"

"Yea. I don't get the joke." And it's clear she doesn't.

"It's not a joke." I sigh heavily before continuing, "You really need to go to church once in a while."

Jen wasn't raised in a church-every-Sunday family like I was. My faith is important to me, and although I don't go to church as religiously as I once did, when I do go, Jen comes along. Granted, she reads the children's Bible, complete with Biblical cartoons accompanying each parable, but she's there and takes part in the service.

In addition to Jen's amazing talents as a human and a partner are her candid acknowledgements of when she finds herself in areas outside her many spheres of expertise. Like here, at this red light, fully believing she has missed the punchline of the Jewish carpenter joke. Quickly, she pieces it all together, drawing deep from those colorful drawings intended for the blank canvas of a child's mind, just starting to learn about God's word.

"Ohhhhhh, I get it…" and I knew this was going to be good, "…the Jewish carpenter is Moses." Before having a chance to react to that gem, she follows it with something just as priceless, "…the guy who built the ark, right?"

I shake my head while she laughs, realizing and admitting she's in over her head—a testament to her religion of honesty. I'm agnostic about whether she's pairing my need for a deluge of relief with a true lack of awareness or if she's being funny on purpose.

Humor is important to me, and Jen makes me laugh, sometimes on purpose and sometimes by just being herself. It may not always be at the most appropriate time or with the most appropriate comment, but it's always when I need it the most.

So if you ever need some comic relief, whether it's truly innocent or intentional, I know a gal.

When's the last time you had a much-needed laugh?

Drive Like Your Kids

If you ever find yourself riding while Jen drives and reads bumper stickers, be forewarned, sometimes she'll randomly smack your forehead.

Well, I suppose it's not random.

And I doubt she'd do it to you.

The first time she did it to me, I didn't heed the sign that it was coming. After that, she did it so predictably that it drove me crazy and I told her to give me a brake. Because every time she sees a street sign that warns "Stop Ahead," she plants her hand across my face to compliantly prevent my head from going anywhere.

There's another sign in our neighborhood that reads, "Drive like your kids live here!" The first time Jen and I came across this sign together, she read it out loud, "Drive like your kids. Live here!" As if the neighborhood was touting itself as an area where its drivers were inexperienced and wouldn't we all love to live in a constant state of fear in this world of vehicular chaos?

I laughed because I had read the sign as it was probably intended, without a pause in the sentence. But it got me to thinking about miscommunication. Jen and I have had quite an assortment of muddled messaging, but it seems that miscommunication isn't a problem just for Jen and me.

I'm sure there were miscommunications back when mobile phones were tin cans and string, but in a world where in-person communication is on the decline, it's not too big of a leap to think misunderstandings are also on the rise. A UCLA study summarized that communication is 7% in the words we use and 93% in voice quality and other nonverbal characteristics.

Many times, the way we read a text or e-mail is not the way the author intended it to be read. This can lead the reader to a different message other than the one intended, possibly resulting in hurt feelings or arguments. While you can't put a price on hurt feelings, a study of 400 U.S. and U.K. corporations estimated employee misunderstandings and miscommunications totaled $37 billion a year (not a typo, that's a *b*).

If we take the time to savor and digest the message rather than spitting it out at first sniff or taste, we can reduce the emotional and financial impacts from miscommunication. If it's a message that affects us emotionally, the counsel we get from more levelheaded people is to take a deep breath and count to 10 before responding. In that short span of time, we can try to think of an alternative interpretation of the message we've received. Partly, this is to create some space between you and your belief, giving your mind and feelings the opportunity to regroup.

If it's a message that didn't land squarely in the field of understanding, it can be as simple as clarifying the intention rather than acting on an assumption. Of course, in the modern age of long-distance communication technologies, many times all we have are words without the amplifying nonverbals. It's harder to put ourselves in other people's shoes when we can't *see* those shoes.

This is all part of adapting to our current environment of modern comms. As we transition to a more high-tech manner of messaging, we need to keep in mind the low-tech message of manners. Something to pass on to our kids, which I don't have, but if I did, I certainly wouldn't drive like them.

What's a written message you misread?

I'll See to It That Mr. Barrett Is Taken Care Of

Immediately after Jen learns that Moses <u>isn't</u> the Jewish carpenter who built the ark, we are back at the funeral home, escorted into a private room to view Dad and his hopefully improved final resting makeup.

Jen might as well have on white gloves and an inspector's clipboard, because if you disappoint Jen once, you have an uphill battle to regain any of her respect. She peers down at Dad's eyebrows and sideburns and points out that they still need to be combed out and cleaned up.

The funeral director takes diligent notes on his clipboard (his is real, Jen's is figurative). Jen, impatient with whatever he's writing, glares at him, "Well?" Her tone of voice ammo is an effective second layer of assault on top of her very aggressive body language. The funeral director looks up from his clipboard on which he was probably just doodling to prevent eye contact with Jen.

Professionally, he tells Jen (it's like I'm literally merely a fly on the wall), "We prefer not to prepare our customers in front of the family. I'll see to it that Mr. Barrett is taken care of with the concerns you have raised."

Clearly, it was a canned and rehearsed phrase from funeral director school. Probably one of those things you learn that you don't imagine you'll ever have to use. Also, Jen is one of those clients you don't imagine you'll ever have to meet.

"I'm not leaving until I see Walter's face and hair fixed."

"Yes, ma'am."

No one moves.

"Well?" Jen's raised eyebrows indicate that movement is expected of at least one of us in the room.

"We prefer not to prepare our customers in front of the family. I'll see to it that Mr. Barrett is taken care of with the concerns you have raised." Wow! It <u>was</u> a rehearsed and canned phrase. (I made that up before, but hearing the exact same words again confirms it.)

"I'm not leaving until I see Walter's face and hair fixed," Jen says again, continuing the copy-and-paste conversation. "So go get your little makeup kit, bring it back here and fix this." Jen waves an open hand over

Dad's face to indicate the "this" that was to be fixed with the "little makeup kit."

When we first arrived, the tissue to my face was to catch the tears of sadness from seeing my dad. Now the tissue is there to catch the tears of laughter from watching Jen defend my dad with the same blunt course of action he would have employed.

I don't typically get pleasure from other people's displeasure, but I admit that I am smiling as I watch the funeral director's shaky hands maneuver the tiny little hairbrush over Dad's eyebrows and sideburns while Jen hovers nearby, evaluating his technique with intense scrutiny.

You can bet your life that we didn't leave that funeral home until the funeral director's work complied with Jen's strict standards.

Dead or alive, you want Jen by your side.

Name a "Jen" in your life.

Officers Can't Be Trusted

From the moment I was alive, I was a daddy's girl. As the daughter of a World War II enlisted man, I spent many an evening listening to Dad's stories from the war. More often than not, the nemesis in his stories were the military officers, bumbling, incompetent fools that they were. These characters played a significant role in my life. They were as real as the monsters under my bed or the knight in shining armor waiting to sweep me off my feet.

Stuggart, Germany.

A phenomenal geographic starting point for European travel. A noble city populated with kindhearted people. It is also my home during my command tour of a small Air Force detachment.

Our military unit is located on the Army's Patch Barracks. The post was originally the German Army's *Kurmärker Kaserne*, a World War II headquarter and barracks for one of their tank regiments. After a brief French colonial troop occupation of the post, American troops took over the facility. After a longer U.S. Army occupation of the post, the U.S. Air Force invaded and seized a small patch on Patch. Having a host country like Germany and a host city like Stuttgart is a more than adequate consolation prize for enduring the misfortune of residing on an Army Post.

Our detachment team has a tight working relationship that allows my unique leadership style to shine. As an officer, I always strive to be more of an approachable human than the gruff drill sergeant type or tyrant leader displayed in the movies or in the life Dad relayed from his time during the war.

Dad was consistent about two things: singing the Army Air Corps song to me each night at bedtime and reminding me that "officers can't be trusted." Growing up with that mantra in my head, when I did become an officer, I sought to be the kind of officer Dad would have trusted.

Taking command of this detachment is a professional honor for me, not only because of the hardship location of Stuttgart but also because of the reputation of the hardworking professionals I am joining. Their preceding reputations are spot on. This is a team that works hard and plays hard. They are patient with me, slowly granting me full permissions for personnel systems where previously I had view-only rights. I care about this team of professionals. I respect the work they do and am truly honored that they trust me, sometimes with very personal information.

The other benefit, or possibly curse, of being a small detachment is that we are all in earshot of each other. Maybe that's why we trust each other, because we have to, because we can't very well hide news we get or give over the phone. Such was the case one Wednesday this past spring.

I hear the phone ring at another desk. Nothing unusual about that, obviously, so I keep working.

I hear our superintendent pick up the phone. Also nothing unusual about that (as I mentioned, we're professionals here; the phone makes a noise, we do something about it).

"Oh, hi, Doctor Perez." I know our chief master sergeant has some medical concerns and has been through a battery of tests. This isn't an unexpected call.

I can hear the chief's monosyllabic responses, indicative of someone in receive mode while the person on the other side of the conversation transmits. Also not an unexpected exchange.

"I'M PREGNANT?"

Ok, this is unexpected.

"How is that possible?"

I suspect the question isn't really about *how* but more of a rhetorical question.

In the pregnant pause that followed (pun intended…I have lots of puns in the oven), I drop everything I am doing and stand by our chief with my hand gently on her shoulder as Doctor Perez gives her the rest of the relevant information.

My brain does a shuttle run between the next nine seconds and the next nine months. Those precious moments will be consumed by telling chief's husband, multiple doctor's appointments, of course a baby shower, possibly some temporary help to bridge the gap during her maternity leave, which of course means we have to get the position description written and posted, then we have to sort through the applicants and pick the one best suited to backfill the chief, our new detachment mom. Oh, and mom-to-be is of an age that makes this a high-risk pregnancy, which of course gives birth to a whole new set of complications.

My mind bounces back and forth between the tasks that will be involved with commanding my detachment and caring for our new detachment mother.

To command, I must wear the uniform of the gruff drill sergeant.

To care, I must uncover the compassionate human.

To lead, I must balance the two.

I labor to refocus my efforts to the present.

Chief's body nervously shakes beneath my hand.

I have never birthed more compassion than I am exerting at this very moment.

I know my role right now is to be there.

For her.

For the baby.

"Ok, doctor. Thank you." An unsteady hand gently places the phone back in its cradle.

The chief looks up at me, her eyes bloodshot, her face red, her body still quivering…from laughter.

"April fools!"

Yea, I should mention that this Wednesday in spring is the first of April.

Hook, line, sinker, weight, bait, boat and oar.

I have been reeled in from my desk to the chief's shoulder. And "Doctor Perez" was another member of our detachment calling from our operating location three hours north.

While I'm embarrassed that I, of all people, have been pranked, I wouldn't do anything differently.

I'm glad I showed compassion and was able to be there for the chief, pregnant or not.

I'm glad the detachment found me approachable enough to prank.

I'm glad it's another day at the office where I am able to laugh.

This is the kind of officer I want to be and this is the kind of workplace I want to work in. One with compassion and caring and a healthy dose of comedy.

I should mention, too, that the same man who told me that officers couldn't be trusted was also the man who instituted April Fools' Day as a national holiday in our household. I suspect he's probably disappointed that I didn't catch the joke soon enough.

I just hope he's proud of the trustworthy officer I tried to become.

What unconventional ways do you make your family proud?

Just Step Over It

There's a fine line between trustworthy and gullible. But it's an invisible line…unlike the line in the aircraft parking areas on Air Force bases. Aircraft on Air Force bases are parked in restricted areas, outlined by a wide red stripe painted around the parking area. To get into the restricted area to your plane or out of the restricted area from your plane, you pass through a narrow entry control point, which is merely a white-painted section in the red border.

From the time we start the transfusion of Air Force blue into our blood, we know that entry or exit to and from a restricted area is done so through the entry control point. Stepping over a <u>red</u> line on Air Force flight lines wins you some face-to-face time with the pavement while a security forces troop, and their loaded weapon, ensures you stay cheek to cheek with the tarmac. Bottom line is you do NOT step over red lines.

Thinking this to be a universal truth, and well indoctrinated by the Air Force, I'm leaving my aircraft after having flown onto a naval air station. I've run the checklists, buttoned up the plane and am ready to depart the restricted area. I walk toward where the entry control point should be but find only more red-painted line. I try another possible entry control point with the same result. More attempts to find a white-painted section breaking up the red outline leave me bouncing around the parking area like a ping-pong ball. Each denial of exit makes me a little more frantic. Well, as frantic as pilots allow ourselves to look.

After shedding a career's worth of cool points, a naval master-at-arms (the Navy version of our Air Force security dudes) drives up in his tricked-out, high-tech patrol vehicle. His crisp Navy uniform is accessorized by a smirk acknowledging the victory of a military-enlisted member having caught an officer of another military branch in the rituals of his own service that are unfamiliar to the invader. The fact that he's caught a pilot creates a bonus trifecta.

He pulls up next to me, looking down from the bow of his tall truck, preparing to confront this Air Force intruder on his nautical turf.

"Having trouble, Lieutenant?" he bellows from the mast of his driver's seat.

The condescension in his voice as he uses my rank is not lost on me. A lieutenant in the Navy is the third commissioned officer rank, what we in the Air Force call "captain." The lieutenant that I am in the Air Force is the first commissioned officer rank. So, in the game of who salutes whom, his lieutenant wins a salute from me, the lower-ranking lieutenant. All this will be fresh bait over beers with his buds later. He won't have to fib one bit to cast his tail about catching and releasing an Air Force fly girl who was trapped by his lines.

Side note: a captain in the Air Force is the third commissioned officer rank, but it's the sixth commissioned officer rank in the Navy, so I make a note that in four years when I make captain in the Air Force, I will call him and condescendingly identify myself as "Captain Barrett," and he will jump to attention thinking I'm a Navy captain. And then I will laugh at revenge for the time the Navy painted me into a restricted area.

But, for now, I am still in the restricted area. And I'm still a lieutenant. And I'm still in the Air Force. So, if I wanna make it to the third commissioned rank, I need this master-at-arm's help.

"How do I get over this red line?"

He exchanges his mask of condescension for one of shock.

"Ma'am? What do you mean?"

"HOW. DO. I. GET. OVER. THIS. RED. LINE?"

Time as an American overseas will teach you that, to be understood, you must simply repeat yourself slowly and more loudly.

Dumfounded, he says, "Ma'am. Just step over it."

Smart ass.

Like it was that simple.

But it was.

Naval air stations, I quickly learn, are less rigid about flight line security. They assume that if you have access to the flight line, you know what you're doing. So when you need to get into or out of a restricted area, you just step <u>over</u> the red painted line.

It dawns on me that I am often so afraid of stepping <u>in</u> it or <u>on</u> it that I hesitate and let inaction gain inertia that can be solved by just stepping <u>over</u> it, whatever "it" may be. This means stepping over the "its" of self-doubt, naysayers, obstacles or a lack of motivation. As a wise internet blogger once said, "The journey of a thousand miles begins with one giant leap for mankind" or something...

So the next time you're stalled on that business proposal you told your boss you already completed, just step over that lie and start writing.

The next time you hesitate to share your feelings with someone, just step over that reluctance and profess your gratitude for them.

The next time you commit to writing a book and the publication date is fast approaching and you just can't seem to get over the it of procrastination, just step over that block and start acting like a writer.

Be vulnerable, take risks, but take that first step.

Here's an "it" you can step over right now:
e-mail me at HeyMo@mobarrett.com
and tell me which story made you laugh,
which story made you learn and which
story made you think.

CPSIA information can be obtained
at www.ICGtesting.com
Printed in the USA
BVHW051405281021
620172BV00011B/480/J